The XX Project

The XX Project

Giving women the skills and confidence to step up in the corporate world

By

Maree Burgess

First published in 2015 by Maree Burgess in Melbourne, Australia.
© Maree Burgess
www.mareeburgess.com

All rights reserved. Except as permitted under the Australian Copyright Act 1968 (for example, a fair dealing for the purposes of study, research, criticism or review), no part of this book may be reproduced, stored in a retrieval system, communicated or transmitted in any form or by any means without prior written permission of the copyright owner, except as provided by international copyright law.

Illustrations by Maree Burgess.
Cover illustration by Matt Emery.
Edited by Stephanie Ayres.

National Library of Australia Cataloguing-in-Publication data:
Author: Maree Burgess
Title: The XX Project: Giving women the skills and confidence to step up in the corporate world.
ISBN: 978-0-6488165-1-5

Subjects: Leadership
             Confidence
             Communication

Disclaimer. The information in this book is provided and sold with the knowledge that the author does not offer any legal or other professional advice. It is not intended to provide specific guidance for particular circumstances and it should not be relied on as the basis for any decision to take action or not take action on any matter that it covers. Readers should obtain professional advice where appropriate, before making any such decision. To the maximum extent permitted by law, the author disclaims all responsibility and liability to any person, arising directly or indirectly from any person taking or not taking action based on the information in this publication.

Contents

Foreword   9

Introduction   11

Don't Just Survive – Thrive   15

Having Confidence and Ability   19

    Being 'purposeful'   19

    When someone has heaps of ability but no belief or confidence in herself.   21

    When someone has heaps of confidence, but quite low abilities in reality   25

    When someone has neither the ability to do their job adequately, nor the confidence to speak up about it 29

Understanding Emotional Intelligence to Build Self-Awareness   33

    If you knew then what you know now – raising your awareness!   33

    The five components of emotional intelligence   35

    How you can build self-awareness by being flexible, perceiving and resourceful   38

Walking Your Talk   51

Present to Desired State 57

For what purpose? Developing a meaning for what we want to achieve   61

Coding your internal and external experiences   66

Those limiting thoughts you may have   70

Our values   76

Being comfortable with change   81

Creating a well formed outcome (putting it all together)   91

It still takes work though   96

Raising Your Awareness of Why You Respond to Things the Way You Do   109

The SCARF model   110

The First Impressions We Make and Building Rapport 119

Building rapport   121

Can We Consciously Create Trust with Someone?   127

The three trust building blocks: capability, communication, and collaboration.   129

Creating trust   133

In Corporations, Who You Know Is as Important as What You Know! 137

Successful mentoring   141

Finding a sponsor   146

Hierarchies, Silos, and Politics   149

In Conclusion   163

Acknowledgments   169

Foreword

When Maree first asked me to review her book, I not only considered it an honour, but I knew that I was in for a treat, and would certainly learn something along the way.

As Maree describes in her forward, the personal motivation behind this book is largely about the desire 'to share', a quality that Maree has in spades, but also one that I believe is essential amongst women today.

Regardless of our personal life stories, for many women, there exists an internal expectation to 'do more'. Yet the benchmarks we set for ourselves, often do, as Maree so aptly describes, sometimes leave us feeling like an 'imposter'.

I hope like me, you will find the very personal stories, insights and resources that Maree has shared within these pages, helpful in gaining the self awareness necessary to achieve that important inner balance.

As I was reading, I reflected on the wisdom of the saying often quoted in song, "no one is getting out of here alive". So it's absolutely all about being present, and finding purpose in the journeys we set for ourselves - sooner than later.

Thank you Maree, for helping make that journey a little easier to understand, and for sharing your experience and wisdom in navigating the way ahead.

Lyn Goodear
Mother, Grandmother, Daughter, Sister, Partner, and CEO, Australian HR Institute

Introduction

Why am I writing this?

- To create a resource for women who want to step up in the world
- To provide a tool to aid in creating gender diversity
- To help women recognise that it's okay to want to be more senior
- To question how we balance our work and our life, and the influence of those around us.

My ideal is a balance between women and men in leadership roles. This will allow for diversity of thinking and better outcomes for organisations. For women to step into meetings and not expect to be the only woman in the room. For women to recognise and mitigate the risk of unconscious bias instilled in us through cultural norms.

I'm passionate about helping women to find their voice, to help other women rather than see them as competition, and to be self-aware and aware of others. This is a book for women, and as such, female terms (she, her, woman) are used predominantly throughout. However, that is not to say that male readers will not also benefit from useful insights into how they too can step up into more senior roles.

What has got me to this point in life, where I am an advocate for balance in the working environment to bring a diversity of thought and perspective into corporations?

For a long time, I worked in jobs I could always like – and did – though I took no initiative in shaping my future. Rather, I let other people tell me what my future would be. I earned good salaries in large multinational companies that impressed my friends and family, but I always felt a bit dissatisfied. I felt like an imposter, as I had this nagging feeling that I just lucked into things without ever choosing my own direction. I was at the mercy of external events and people.

I came to the conclusion that I really didn't like what I was doing, and my strengths and skill base were being eroded because of that.

So, I started working in the areas of my strengths and loving what I did. And I made sure that all my decisions were well thought through and focused on what I loved to do, whom I liked working with, and my personal strengths.

You can do this as well.

If you do not change direction, you may end up where you are heading.

—Lao Tzu

Don't Just Survive – Thrive

One of the biggest reasons why we aren't seeing more women move into leadership roles is a lack of self-awareness. The 'expertise and mindset' model below shows the significant differences between being *unaware* and being *self-aware*. I'm assuming if you are reading this that you fall into the top half of this model.

Figure 1: Expertise and Mindset

	EXPERTISE	VALUE		MINDSET
SELF AWARE				
THRIVE	SOUGHT	INVESTED	100	Living to serve
	POSITIONED	ENERGISED	60	Everything is effortless
	VALUED	ENGAGED	40	Inner conviction of self
	ACCEPTED	CAPABLE	20	Comfortably numb
SURVIVE	TOLERATED	CHALLENGED	-40	Bored to tears
	IGNORED	STRESSED	-60	Pushing s#@t up hill
	AVOIDED	CATATONIC	-100	Self sabotaging
UNAWARE				

If organisations were filled with women and men who valued being *invested* at 100% and had a mindset of *living to serve*, imagine the success that would be achieved.

Focusing on building a diverse, balanced organisation filled with trusted individuals whose expertise is valued, positioned, and sought after, and who themselves feel engaged, energised, and invested in their abilities, will help to create a workforce that operates above the line and *thrives*.

When I show this model to clients I find they can identify either themselves or their team somewhere on the ladder.

When individuals are operating below the line, they are *surviving*. Their expertise is avoided, ignored, or tolerated.

When a person's expertise is *avoided*, it is often because they do not have the necessary skills to do their job effectively. Perhaps they have fallen into a role that doesn't suit them because they don't know what their strengths are. They have poor productivity, and they are under considerable stress from the expectations of those around them to lift their game.

When a person's expertise is *ignored*, they are often stressed out as they try to do work that may be beyond their skill set. They madly try to keep up, but still feel ignored. They may ask for help in ways that aren't noticed.

When a person's expertise is *tolerated*, they aren't raising too many alarm bells as to what they are or are not doing; however, they aren't operating at the expected levels for their role. This may be because their skills are lacking and they find their role too challenging, or it may be that they feel unchallenged or bored by doing the same old thing over and over.

At the mid-point, when a person's expertise is *accepted*, they are on par with what is expected for their role. They are capable of doing everything required, they feel very comfortable, and they know what is expected day to day. This is a danger zone, as they are very much in their comfort zone. They may become complacent and do no more than is absolutely required.

When a person's expertise is *valued*, they are kicking goals by doing and achieving more than expected in their role. They are leading and creating. They have a real belief in their abilities, a good understanding of their strengths and values, and an inner conviction of self.

When a person's expertise is *positioned*, they are energised and find everything effortless. They are in flow and thriving in their role. Their abilities are noticed beyond their own team, and they are likely to find that more senior leaders are seeking to sponsor them into other roles and areas.

When a person's expertise is *sought*, they are shooting the lights out. They are invested in the organisation and living to serve. They may feel everything is 'easy', yet they are still challenged and always on the lookout for opportunities to stretch themselves. They know what their strengths are and use those in their role. They are doing far more than expected and truly stepping up in their leadership.

This book will provide you with the tools and knowledge you need to step up into the higher levels of this model, and become instrumental in creating change and bringing much-needed diversity to your organisation.

Having Confidence and Ability

Being 'purposeful'

The Oxford Dictionary definition for *purposeful* is 'having or showing determination or resolve'. Being purposeful is the result of both high confidence and high ability.

Purposeful women are generally sought after for roles and can become the 'go to' people to manage complex issues, special projects or sensitive work. They have a high self-awareness of their abilities, strengths and beliefs, as well as knowing the areas where they are not so strong. They are aware of others and tuned in to what is going on around them.

Purposeful women look the part. They walk and talk confidently, and have the ability and expertise to back it up. They are accountable and committed to reaching the right outcomes. They are consultative and involve others in determining direction. They understand what high-performance teams can achieve, and create these when they lead or are part of a team.

Purposeful women have often built their own successful practice or business from the ground up. They build strong, trusting relationships with clients and focus on the best outcomes for them.

It's a joy to be in the hands of a purposeful woman. Her confidence gives you confidence that this (whatever 'this' is) will work out well.

Figure 2 shows the Confidence/Ability Model. 'Purposeful' sits in the quadrant between high confidence and high ability.

Chances are, you or some women you know may fall into one of the other three quadrants (Poser, Problem or Potential). Let's consider what these mean and what is required to move into the purposeful quadrant.

Figure 2: Confidence/Ability Model

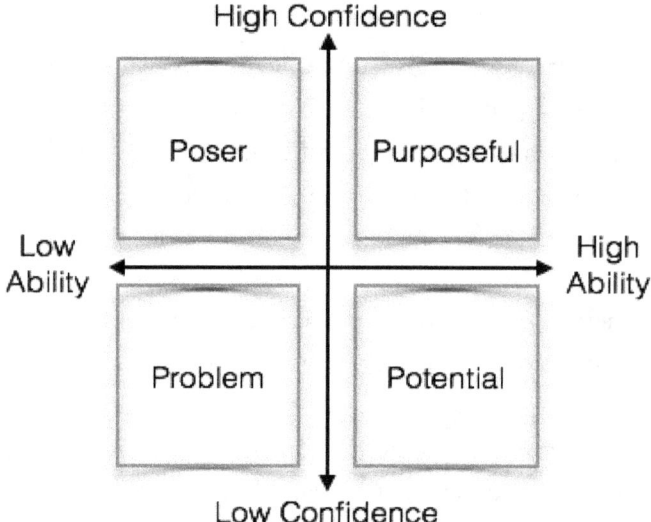

When someone has heaps of ability but no belief or confidence in herself.

How many times have you worked with someone who was incredible in their role, yet didn't believe in themselves or have the confidence to apply for different or more senior roles? You can recognise their *potential*, but they cannot.

In reality that person may feel like an imposter, afraid that they will be found out for what they don't know. By building belief in their abilities and backing it up with evidence, you can give that person more confidence and help them to step up into their role or even apply for a promotion.

I've worked with many women who were outstanding at what they did, but wrote off their accomplishments as something 'anyone could do'.

It's like when you respond to a compliment with 'this old thing', or 'yes, but…' Just say 'thank you' and accept the compliment. We don't have to put ourselves down all the time.

This lack of confidence spills over into what others think of you. Not only will you probably not apply for that more senior role, but even if you do you are unlikely to get it – because you have already set others' expectations of you at the same low level as your own.

I once worked with a woman, Anna (not her real name), who was acting in a senior role while the position was advertised, and it was taking a while to fill. I asked if she had applied for the role and was surprised when she said no. She said she didn't feel she had the necessary experience or qualifications for the role, even though at that time she had already 'acted' in the role for over three months.

This isn't an unfamiliar scenario. We often feel that we don't have the necessary 'something' to perform a certain role. Or we can't tick off every single criterion included in a role description. Actually, it's a known fact that the criteria listed in a role description are a wish list – there is no expectation that someone will arrive being able to do everything. And if they did, it may even rule them out for being 'over-qualified', or the hirer might fear that they will become bored and leave quickly.

This almost happened to me recently when I was applying for a large chunk of work that was a perfect fit for my business, that I was passionate about, and that I desperately wanted to do. The employer felt that this was so similar to what I had already been doing that I would not find the work challenging and would quickly become bored. Fortunately for them and for me, I was able to convince them otherwise.

The irony for Anna is that she ended up being very disappointed with the calibre of the person who finally filled the role, and to whom she had to report. He was inexperienced and a poor people leader.

Figure 2 explains how this occurs. People in the low confidence/high ability quadrant have *potential*, and can certainly move into the high confidence/high ability quadrant by focusing on their strengths, becoming aware of their beliefs and building their confidence to become purposeful.

I have worked with many women to help them move into the purposeful quadrant. It's like enhancing or tuning a high performance vehicle to get superb results. There are a number of ways to build confidence in your abilities, or help someone else build confidence in theirs.

Here are some suggestions:

- Watch the Amy Cuddy TED talk – she talks about 'faking it until you are it'.
- Learn how to create internal resourceful states for yourself or others – in times of need, they can be used to create a feeling of confidence. See the chapter 'How you can build self-awareness by being flexible, perceiving and resourceful' for more on this.
- Create well-formed outcomes and really dig down to the purpose for which you want to achieve them – this will set up a direction to follow.

My questions are:

- Are you constantly putting yourself down?
- Are you frustrated with someone in your team who needs a confidence injection to reach their potential?
- When people tell you that you are great at what you do, do you water it down and say things like 'I don't do anything special', or 'anyone could do that'? Can you accept a compliment graciously? More importantly, do you believe in your strengths?
- What are you doing about stepping up or helping someone else step up?
- When you look at a role, do you focus on those attributes you don't think you have, or the value and experience you can bring to the overall role?

One of my favourite quotes, written by Marianne Williamson in her book 'A Return to Love: Reflections on the Principles of a Course in Miracles', summarises this nicely:

> Our deepest fear is not that we are inadequate. Our deepest fear is that we are powerful beyond measure. It is our light, not our darkness that most frightens us. We ask ourselves, Who am I to be brilliant, gorgeous, talented, fabulous? Actually, who are you not to be? You are a child of God. Your playing small does not serve the world. There is nothing enlightened about shrinking so that other people won't feel insecure around you. We are all meant to shine, as children do. We were born to make manifest the glory of God that is within us. It's not just in some of us; it's in everyone. And as we let our own light shine, we unconsciously give other people permission to do the same. As we are liberated from our own fear, our presence automatically liberates others.

When someone has heaps of confidence, but quite low abilities in reality

How do you manage that and even give her feedback?

Working with someone who is supremely confident but doesn't yet have the ability to do what needs to be done can also be a problem. While you don't want to destroy her confidence, it is important to make her aware of the gaps in her abilities.

If this sounds like you, you need to understand that confidence without ability (the skills to back it up) could end badly for you in the long run and may create a 'personal brand' that will be difficult to change in the future.

Have you ever been driving and mistakenly put the car into Reverse instead of Drive? This is how it can feel when someone is so confident that they charge ahead without necessarily checking that they are going in the right direction.

An activity that I run in team workshops involves completing a toothpicks puzzle. Participants are instructed to wait until I am beside them to do the exercise. Sometimes I will go to stand beside the next participant only to find that they have already completed the activity. One person, when it was pointed out that they were instructed to wait, said, 'when I see the answer I just go for it!' Whether they had completed the activity correctly or not is immaterial, as the learning didn't happen until everyone had finished. Being supremely confident is great… unless you end up heading in the wrong direction.

But maybe it is not that you have low ability. It could be that you are just in the wrong role, trying to do something you're not good at and putting on a confident face about it.

I have found myself in this situation. Many years ago, I was working for a large corporation and had been progressively moving away from what I was good at and loved (working with people), as my boss at the time didn't understand my strengths, and if I'm being honest, neither did I. I didn't have the self-awareness to understand my strengths or articulate what was wrong.

Participating in a culture change program and completing a 360-degree survey totally opened my eyes. What I identified as being good at and what everyone I invited to complete my survey identified that I was good at matched. Ironically, none of these things were part of my role at the time. This led to a complete career change and the establishment of my coaching practice.

Let's refer back to Figure 2. People with high confidence and low ability are known as *posers*. This sounds harsh, but we've all experienced this type of person. They can move into the 'purposeful' quadrant by focusing on the areas of their role they need to develop, becoming aware of what they may not be doing well, listening to and acting on any feedback (and making it known that they are open to receiving feedback), and building their abilities to become purposeful.

When I have worked with women who operate out of this quadrant, raising their self-awareness is one of the first areas I focus on. I put the spotlight on them and highlight any flaws. The first step is to recognise what may need enhancing, and create an action plan to achieve that.

Here are some suggestions:

- Complete a 360-degree feedback survey, and ask people whose opinion you value to provide honest feedback.
- Tell people that you want feedback on your performance (and be willing to listen without judgment when they give it).
- Complete a strengths inventory to determine where your strengths lie, then determine if that matches what you are expected to do in your role.

My questions are:

- Are people giving you feedback, or cautioning you about what you have been doing?
- Do you know if your role leverages your strengths?
- Do you find that work assignments are handed out to other people?
- Do you have a development plan that has been created in conjunction with your boss?

And as Dr Seuss says,

> You have brains in your head
> You have feet in your shoes
> You can steer yourself in any direction you choose
> You're on your own
> And you know what you know
> You are the one who'll decide where to go.

When someone has neither the ability to do their job adequately, nor the confidence to speak up about it

When someone you work with has low confidence *and* their abilities aren't that great, you may find it difficult to trust them to do their work adequately. This also creates trust issues with other team members and can cause frustration for everyone involved. The person's coping mechanisms start to fail and they may find it very difficult to become motivated. Mistakes are made, and often hidden, and suddenly there is a snowball effect.

If this is you, you're in a tough situation and you just can't see your way forward. You definitely don't look forward to coming to work each day. It's like trying to walk through treacle, feeling stuck and unsure how to overcome it.

If you are in a team with people like this, it can damage team trust and create hostility or even anger as some team members carry more of the load and feel that others are incapable of doing their job.

If you are a leader, being aware of what is going on with your team members is essential to prevent organisational health and safety concerns.

If someone in your team has low ability and low confidence, you need to work out what they require to build up their confidence to the point that they feel able to speak up and ask for help. If you know what is needed, are there specific areas of development you can recommend?

Many years ago, I worked in a team with an underperforming team member. Our leader didn't address this issue and that led to general frustration from everyone on the team. It created trust issues as doubts arose about what this person was capable of doing, and no-one wanted to work with them. The person's confidence was eroded and they felt they couldn't speak up. It ended up with them taking extended stress leave and eventually leaving the organisation. It was a very sad outcome for a situation that could have been handled much better.

Referring back to Figure 2, people with low confidence and low ability are known as *problems*. We have all experienced these people, and while it may be a challenge and require extensive effort, they too can move towards the purposeful quadrant. Like posers, they can make improvements by focusing on the areas of their role they need to develop, becoming aware of what they may not be doing well, listening to and acting on any feedback (and making it known that they are open to receiving feedback), and building their abilities. They also need encouragement and support from their leader and team members to build their confidence.

This isn't a quadrant I work in often, as it requires remedial support and sometimes counselling, but when I do, raising self-esteem is one of the first areas I focus on. It's like wrapping a warm towel around them and making them feel safe and supported before moving to more tangible areas of development. The first step is to recognise which quadrant they are in and create an action plan to support them.

Here are some suggestions:

- Recognise that this person is in this quadrant (low ability and low confidence).
- Find ways to help them build their self-esteem.
- Work with them to identify gaps in their abilities, and then create an action plan to fill these gaps.

- If personal issues are reducing their confidence and, in turn, diminishing their abilities, check if they need external support such as counselling.
- Learn how to give good feedback that targets specific behaviours or outcomes, not personality – then give the feedback.

My questions are:

- Are you frustrated with someone in your team who needs a confidence injection to reach their potential?
- Are there people you work with currently who are at risk?
- What can you do to build up someone's abilities?
- Are you in this quadrant and not sure how to get out of it? Identify one thing you can do to get help.

Low self-confidence isn't a life sentence.
Self-confidence can be learned, practiced, and mastered
– just like any other skill.
Once you master it, everything in your life will change for the better.

—Barrie Davenport

Understanding Emotional Intelligence to Build Self-Awareness

If you knew then what you know now – raising your awareness!

'Emotional Intelligence' refers to a psychological theory developed by Peter Salovey and John Mayer in 1990:

> Emotional intelligence is the ability to perceive emotions, to access and generate emotions so as to assist thought, to understand emotions and emotional knowledge, and to reflectively regulate emotions so as to promote emotional and intellectual growth.

Daniel Goleman used this term in his bestselling 1995 book 'Emotional Intelligence: Why It Can Matter More than IQ'. At a basic level, emotional intelligence relies on two things: self-awareness, and awareness of others.

Have you ever spent time with someone who makes you feel that they really see you and really hear you?

That person has the ability to be totally aware of you. Their awareness of themselves and others is high, and if you asked other people about that person they would probably say the same thing.

Developing this awareness is like becoming clear sighted (perhaps you have new glasses) after having blurry vision for years. When things become clear, you have a different view of what is going on around you.

Increasing self-awareness is about understanding who you are. What are your strengths and weaknesses? What do you value? What are your beliefs?

What is your identity? Knowing even a little more about each of these improves your ability to continue to grow and develop, and have the flexibility to change as required.

The higher your self-awareness, the better your understanding of where you add value and how you impact others.

Conversely, lack of self-awareness can lead to low confidence and misunderstanding of strengths and values.

If I know who I am and I know who you are, then we can communicate. Having an understanding of what makes me tick *and* what makes you tick helps in all sorts of interactions we have together: working together, negotiating, influencing, building high performance teams. Awareness gives me choice in how I interact with you to create the best outcomes.

How can we strengthen our self-awareness and awareness of others to create that same feeling in others when we interact? How do we make them feel that we really 'see' them?

The following descriptions are adapted from Goleman's 1998 Harvard Business Review article, 'Emotional Intelligence: What Makes a Leader?'

The five components of emotional intelligence

Self-awareness

Self-awareness relates to our ability to understand our personal moods, emotions and drives, as well as their effect on others. High self-awareness creates self-confidence, the ability to self-assess, and the ability to laugh at ourselves. When we are self-aware, we monitor our emotional state and can correctly identify and name our emotions. We have a strong understanding of who we are.

Self-regulation

Self-regulation is how we manage our internal state by controlling or redirecting disruptive impulses and moods, and our ability to suspend judgment and to pause and think before acting. People with high levels of self-regulation have integrity, are considered trustworthy, and are comfortable with ambiguity and open to change. Self-regulation allows us to be aware of how we are responding to events or people.

Internal motivation

One who is internally motivated is passionate about work (or life) for internal reasons, such as prioritising what is important in life, possessing a thirst or curiosity for learning, taking joy in doing something, or enjoying the flow of being immersed in an activity. Internal motivation creates a drive to pursue and achieve goals, and fosters optimism even in the face of failure. External motivation comes from external rewards such as money or status.

Empathy

Empathy is the ability to understand the emotional makeup of other people and the skill to treat people according to their emotional reactions. People with high levels of empathy have cross-cultural sensitivity, a service mindset for clients, and a high ability to build and retain talent in organisations.

Social skills

People with good social skills are proficient in managing relationships and building networks, and have a strong ability to find common ground and build rapport. The hallmarks of good social skills are effectiveness in leading change, persuasiveness, and expertise in building and leading teams.

There are various ways to increase your self-awareness and awareness of others.

A 360-degree feedback survey is a relatively simple way of opening up what you know about yourself and finding out what others know about you.

The Johari Window, developed by Joseph Luft and Larry Ingram in 1963, is another way to understand the importance of building awareness of yourself and others. The model describes how to become aware of what you allow into your public space and what you hide from others, and also to find out what others know about you that you may not know about yourself. The model suggests that the more shared information that exists about members of a team, the more effective the team is in achieving its outcomes. The bigger our public zone, the easier it is to deal with issues, continuously improve, and give the best possible value to the team.

Figure 3: The Johari window

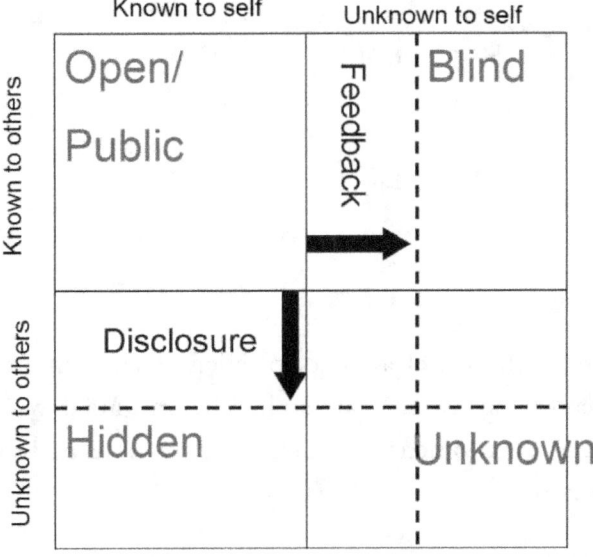

How you can build self-awareness by being flexible, perceiving and resourceful

Figure 4: The three components of self-awareness

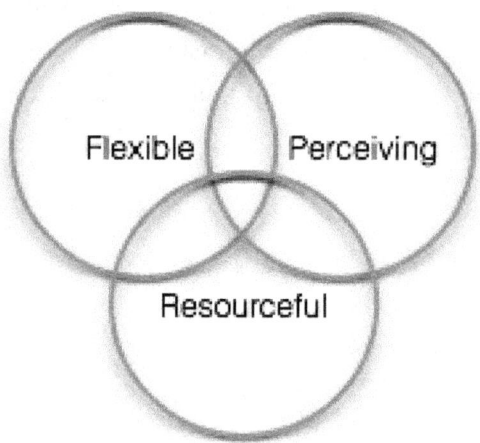

Being flexible

Have you ever played with pipe cleaners or plasticine? You can create infinite different shapes because they are so bendy. Imagine if you could be this flexible and, at any moment, be exactly what you needed to be to achieve the best outcome.

The Oxford Dictionary definition of flexible is to be 'able to be easily modified to respond to altered circumstances', or '(of a person) ready and able to change so as to adapt to different circumstances'.

Behavioural flexibility means that you have the ability to secure a response from another person by varying your own behaviour. It means you have a range of responses to any given situation rather than having the same habitual, and therefore limiting, responses.

I sometimes ask people for the definition of insanity. The response I'm looking for is: 'repeating the same thing over and over and expecting a different result'!

If you get the same response from people when you interact with them (and it's not useful), maybe it's time to try something different – and achieve a different result. For example, maybe you have a tense relationship with a teammate and you believe that they don't respect you or value your opinion. Think about how you usually interact with them. Are you defensive, or accusatory, or do you just not share your opinion (the silent treatment)? Now think about what you could do differently in your interactions to break out from your habitual, and maybe limiting, responses.

Many years ago I had a particularly challenging relationship with a member of a committee I chaired. I perceived that Bob didn't value the opinions of anyone else on our committee and went out of his way to be difficult and challenging. This opinion was shared by most of the committee. As a result our meetings became progressively more difficult and we achieved very little.

After learning about the need to have more behavioural flexibility I decided to try it out with Bob. I changed how I responded to him during meetings (previously my body language had my body angled away from him, I totally minimised eye contact, and I enforced strict guidelines about how long anyone could talk about a particular issue to limit what he could say).

The small changes I made were to increase eye contact, face Bob directly and actively listen, and respond back indicating that I was seeking to understand what he was saying. I also asked challenging questions (rather than trying to rush the conversation and move onto the next agenda item) to get him to really consider what he was saying.

Over the next few weeks and months, Bob's behaviour began to change, which created a bit of a snowball effect with other committee members as their behaviours also began to change. We ended up achieving a lot of great things through that committee. And while I personally still don't like Bob, we found that we could work together constructively. My ability to respond differently, and get a different result, certainly contributed to that outcome.

A suggestion to develop your behavioural flexibility:

Try a Self-Edit. This focuses on reviewing your day as is, noting all the areas that didn't go so well, then reviewing the day again and imagining it running seamlessly with great interactions. This creates continuous improvement because at an unconscious level, your mind cannot tell the difference between fact and fiction. The next time this interaction occurs, in your mind you will have already responded differently. Let's look at the Self-Edit in a little more detail.

Self-Edit (memory management for performance enhancement)

Self-edits are a tool for use in everyday life. Self-edits allow for self-feedback and correction, allowing you to enhance your performance in the context of your choosing, and raise your self-awareness.

You can select areas from your everyday life that you wish to capitalise on, as well as things you wish to change. You get the opportunity to rerun your day, and, knowing what you know, to do things differently. You cannot change how others responded, but you can review your responses and adjust your emotional/ behavioural responses.

Mistakes are not learning experiences unless you learn. Self-editing is a tool that converts mistakes into learning experiences. When you adjust your attention to become more aware during a self-edit, you avoid the circular thinking that keeps you revisiting moments of pain, shame and embarrassment.

Method

1) Run through the chosen time period (for example, a day), paying special attention to those events that didn't turn out as you would have liked.
2) Run through the time period again, this time constructing how the events could have played out if your behaviour had been different.
3) Lock these changes in by running through the time period again, as if it had gone seamlessly.
4) Now think of a time in the future where a similar scenario is likely to occur. Imagine it runs in the same seamless way as in Step 3.

As a variation on the self-edit, John Grinder (co-creator of Neuro-Linguistic Programming [NLP]) suggests that each night before going to sleep, you review your day and create three different ways you could have responded to events. This way you will automatically build up your behavioural flexibility, and you will discover that you respond more appropriately to the world around you.

My questions are:

- Have you thought about people you have a difficult relationship with? How are you currently responding?
- How could you respond differently to create a more constructive relationship?

Perceiving yourself and others

There is an old saying, 'you can't really understand another person's experience until you've walked a mile in their shoes.'

The ability to step into another's shoes creates more awareness about yourself, and about others. Your ability to take on different perspectives and different points of view enhances the description you have for something. Your ideas or experiences are greatly affected by the point of view or perspective from which you consider them.

There are three 'perceptual positions'. These refer to the points of view taken when considering the relationship between yourself and another person.

In first position: You are looking at the world out of your own eyes; hearing with your own ears; and feeling, tasting and smelling using all your senses. You are associated with your own point of view, beliefs, and assumptions.

In second position: You are experiencing another's psychological state, perception, and viewpoint through your own senses. To take second position, you must associate with the other person's point of view, beliefs and assumptions, and see the world through their eyes. You are in the other person's 'shoes'.

In third position: You are acting as an observer, watching what is happening, and possibly forming opinions about the subject of observation. You are dissociated from the relationship between yourself and the other person, observing the interactions of these two people.

When you move from position to position, never go directly from first the second or second to first, as this can cause contamination of either position. Always go to second position via third, and return from second to first via third.

The ability to step into another's shoes creates more awareness about yourself, and about others.

Your ability to shift perceptual positions means that communication is enhanced and the possibility of future cooperation is created.

The ability to switch points of view and take into account multiple perspectives of a situation or experience enriches the information you are able to tap into.

We can often spend our lives inhabiting one perceptual position (and not necessarily first position), which means we are limited in the amount of information we can collect and use and limited in our flexibility in responding to others.

With practice you can learn to live in first position as your home base, and move to third and second position to gather information in your interactions with others.

Working with other people (in any role or any industry) involves gathering as much information as you can about the people around you and their needs. It involves understanding their values, their beliefs, and their perceptions of themselves. Being able to move through the three perceptual positions will help you build rapport with people more readily, clarify your understanding of their perspectives, and help you understand what you *don't* know about them.

Here are some suggestions:

- Think about someone you regularly interact with and practise moving from first position, to third position (observer), to second position, back to third, and then to first position (back to you).
- Think of a challenging meeting you have to attend and put yourself fully into first position by imagining that the people from that meeting are here right now and you are looking at them through your eyes.
  Now view the relationship as an observer from third position. Observe the interaction of the attendees of the meeting, including yourself, as if you were observing a video of the meeting.
  Now imagine that you are in another attendee's shoes, in second position. Look at yourself from their eyes. Assume the perspectives, beliefs, and assumptions of that attendee as if you were them for a moment. Repeat for the other attendees.
  Review the information you have gained.
- Notice how taking different perceptual positions changes your perception of an experience.

My questions are:

- Have you ever been aware of stepping into another's shoes?
- In the exercises above, what did you notice? Did you develop new awareness about yourself, the audience, or the meeting?
- How could moving between perceptual positions and building rapport help in your interactions with others?
- How could it help you in the quest for a more senior role?

You just get it – now you are resourceful!

Have you ever experienced the feeling that for the first time in a long time, everything is really clear? You really 'get' what is going on, and everything you do just hums?

You are in a resourceful state.

Being resourceful means having a state of mind that is useful for the interaction you are having and includes thoughts, emotions, and physiology (including breathing and posture), all expressed in the moment.

A presupposition I use in coaching and training others is that we all have all the resources required to achieve our outcomes. We have brilliant brains, bodies that perform amazing functions in every moment, and an incredible ability to see, hear, taste, feel, smell, and communicate.

We have everything we need to live highly successful lives.

Often, though, we haven't tuned into our resources, or we may have a set of limiting beliefs that prevent us from gaining full access. This means that in a lot of ways we exist in unresourceful states, and this is why we sometimes struggle to achieve the life or outcomes we want. American writer Ambrose Bierce eloquently observed that

> [a] person who doubts himself is like a man who would enlist in the ranks of his enemies and bear arms against himself. He makes his failure certain by himself being the first person to be convinced of it.

Any state that can be perceived as negative can be considered unresourceful, including worry (about what's going to happen tomorrow, or what happened yesterday), anger (at yourself or at others), fear, tiredness, blame, and many more. These can present in very obvious ways, such as a panic attack, or more subtle ways, such as worrying that your boss is angry with you about something, but not knowing what it is and spending hours wondering what's wrong.

Because my approach with anyone I work with is to presuppose that the resources are already in place to achieve whatever it is they want to achieve, it's a matter of reminding them of how to tap into these resources.

When you are resourceful, you feel in control, calm, and in flow; you have a heightened awareness of what is going on around you and others; and your mind can create options or make clear decisions. You feel resourceful at all levels – physical, emotional, and mental.

So how do you attain that place? And when you are being unresourceful, how do you create that self-awareness of how you are being and what is happening around you? How do you switch to a state of resourcefulness?

An NLP technique called 'Circle of Excellence' anchors desirable patterns of behaviour into our physiology, which can then be used in all aspects of our lives. This technique provides a useful resource for becoming more centred and balanced as a human being.

The thoughts and feelings that we hold as we move through the world tremendously affect whether or not we operate from a 'centre of strength' or not. By building and storing a 'state of resourcefulness', we can choose to operate from this state.

I often work with people who want to become effective public speakers.

Some people are terrified to get up to stand in front of a group, and instructing them on how to create a 'Circle of Excellence' is particularly beneficial. In the case of public speaking, a resourceful state may be one of confidence, assertiveness, and clear thinking.

Here is one way to create a resourceful state:

1) Identify a resourceful state. What state would you like to have available to use? Think about times when you felt powerful, creative, or composed; or any resourceful state where you felt balanced and centred. Find a state that will allow you to act with more of your capacities and skills. What is a resourceful state for you, in which you would feel at your best?

2) Now place an imaginary circle in front of you on the floor and imagine that circle represents your resourceful state. What does the identified resourceful state look like? What does it feel like, and sound like? As you stand outside the circle, recall a time when you had all the qualities of that state you would like to have available now, and in the future. As you fully recreate that experience, notice how you feel, what you say to yourself, what you see, and how you hold your body when you possess these abilities. Amplify this. When you have completely recreated that state, step into the circle and experience it fully.

3) From inside the circle, you will be experiencing and possessing all the qualities and abilities of that state. As you do, fully hear what you say to yourself, see what you look like, and notice how you feel. Anchor this state even more fully by pinching your thumb and your pointer finger, then releasing them.

4) Now step out. Step out cleanly and discretely, leaving the circle intact. Shake that state off.

5) Access the resourceful state again. Practise stepping into the circle

of excellence and being there in that state. Repeat this twice more to continue to build this resourceful state. Continue to anchor to the pinching gesture each time you enter the circle. Fully shake the state off when you step outside the circle.

6) Finally, test the anchor. Without considering your resourceful state, step into the circle and see what you notice. (You should experience the state as you had built it.)

7) You now have access to that state whenever you want it - simply by imagining that circle, or accessing the gesture you anchored the state to (pinching your thumb and your pointer finger).

My questions are:

- When will it be useful for you to have access to a resourceful state?
- Have you considered anchoring states as you experience them?

Walking Your Talk

When you walk your talk, you are congruent: what you say matches what you believe, what you know to be true, and what you do.

Congruence means saying and doing what you believe in the moment, being straightforward and honest, and saying what is true, even if it is unpleasant and not what you think others want to hear.

People intuitively sense when you are not being congruent, even if it is only to avoid hurting their feelings. When you are incongruent to temporarily smooth over a rough situation, or take the pain out of an unpleasant encounter, sooner or later it will catch up with you and the relationship will be damaged or destroyed.

Sometimes we may believe we are being congruent when we are not. We may be in conflict internally without necessarily recognizing that to be the case.

This is where our brain – or perhaps more accurately, our *brains* – become involved.

There is significant evidence that as well as the brain in our head; we have at least two other 'brains' – one in our heart and one in our gut. According to Marvin Oka and Grant Soosalu, founders of a new field called 'mBraining',

> The latest scientific research shows you have three brains! You have complex, adaptive and fully functional neural networks or 'brains' in your heart, your gut and your head.

These have the same constructs as the brain in our head: neurons, synapses, and so on. Building alignment between our three brains creates authenticity and congruence. When they are aligned, all moving and thinking in sync, they work like an open freeway with no stoppages or blockages – the traffic just moves at the right speed and pace. This is very exciting, as it allows us to tap into our brains to achieve great results.

Oka and Soosalu's mBraining uses the latest neuroscience findings about our multiple brains to tap into our innate intelligence. This allows us to increase our intuitive abilities and make wiser decisions in our daily lives.

Oka and Soosalu have developed the Multiple Brain Integration Technique (mBIT), a set of practical ways to tap into our brains, balance the autonomic nervous system (ANS), and enable open communication between the brains in our head, heart, and gut. This creates balance, alignment, and congruence.

Have you ever wanted to do something but that voice in your head kept preventing you from making the first move? That's your head brain trying to tell you something.

Have you ever gone ahead with something even though it didn't feel quite right, and found that it didn't work out? That's your gut brain trying to tell you something.

Or have you experienced those moments when your heart just wasn't into it, whatever 'it' was? That's your heart brain trying to tell you something.

In all of these situations, the messages from your brains are not in alignment.

Many years ago when I was desperate to find work, I applied for a 'perfect' coaching role at a small boutique company. I was excited to be interviewed several times; I presented to them and even worked in their office for a day completing a series of tasks. The interview process took about three months, and halfway through the process I started to have doubts about the organisation, particularly the business owner.

Finally I was offered the role and actually declined it, for many reasons. The owner talked me around, and I decided to start working on a part-time basis. But my heart just wasn't in it and I left after 11 months. I wasn't listening to my head *or* my heart. My gut, which was operating out of fear (I needed work for the money), became the dominant brain in this decision.

Our ability to align our three brains is critical to achieve greater wisdom, success and happiness in a world of massive change. When your head, heart, and gut are fully aligned, you are in flow and congruent.

Having learnt about mBraining and become an mBIT coach several years ago, I now incorporate mBIT into my programs with leaders to help them create internal congruence and increase self-awareness and awareness of others.

Recently one of my coaching clients experienced a completely new mindset following an mBIT session. She had been experiencing doubt in her own abilities and was not speaking up during meetings, which meant that her valuable advice and experience was not being shared. Her feedback to me was that following our session she stepped straight into another meeting and behaved more assertively than she usually would, which led to a great outcome (and a more senior role).

Here is a suggestion to practise creating internal alignment:

- We can communicate with our three brains by breathing. Simply inhaling and exhaling at a regular pace brings your autonomic nervous system into balance.

    Sit quietly with your feet flat on the floor and your hands in your lap. Close your eyes, let your body soften and relax, and gently breathe in for a count of six seconds, and out for a count of six seconds. Keep repeating this.

    Once you are breathing in an even, balanced rhythm, focus your breath in your heart area and just notice what you notice. Keep breathing in and out for a few moments, keeping your awareness on your heart.

    Then, imagine moving your breath to your head and filling your head space with that breath. Breathe in and out focusing on your head brain and imagining the air filling that space. Again, just notice what you notice.

    Now move your breath to your gut. Breathe in and out, focusing on filling your gut space with your breath, noticing what you notice.

    Continue to move your breath between your heart, head and gut and continue to focus on what you notice as you move to each. Do this for about five minutes. Pause, open your eyes and reflect on how you feel.

My questions are:

- Are you in conflict with your thoughts – your head is saying one thing and your heart or gut another?
- Do you avoid acting on your goals and plans or find it difficult to be motivated?
- Do you ever experience frustration, depression, anger, or anxiety?

Creating alignment between your head, heart and gut brains may reduce any of these.

Present to Desired State

Imagine you've just arrived in Melbourne on a plane. You are waiting in the taxi rank at Tullamarine Airport and finally a taxi is in front of you. You get in and the driver says, 'Where to?' What do you say? What would happen if you said, 'I don't want to go to Bendigo, I don't want to go to Brunswick, and I know I don't want to go to Brighton'? What does the taxi driver do? Nothing. She has no idea where to take you.

Is your career like this? You have a good idea where you don't want to go, or what you don't want to do, but you are unclear of where you *do* want to go.

Working with your present state (where you are now) and determining what you desired state is (where you want to get to) is called 'P to D'.

Understanding your present state is just as important as knowing your desired state. It's like discovering where the 'x' is on a treasure map and trying to work out how to get to it. To find the 'x', obviously you have to work out where the 'you are here' mark is as well.

Often the most difficult part of planning ahead is working out what it is you want to achieve. Once you know what your desired state is, then it is just a process of working out the steps to get there, or what is preventing you from getting there.

Figure 5: Present to Desired State

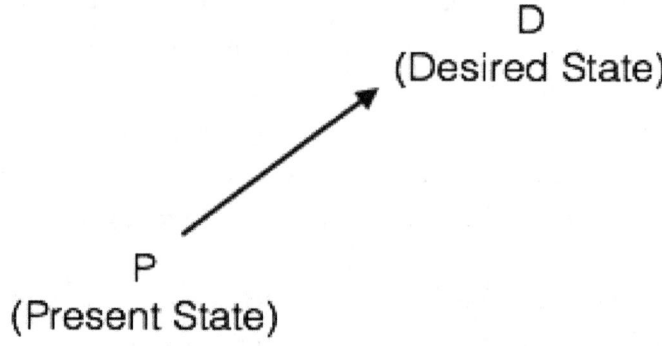

Once you have a good idea what your desired state looks like, you have to determine the purpose (why you want to achieve it), develop the commitment, and build the belief to get there.

You may know your purpose for reaching that desired state, and have the commitment, but not the belief. Without belief, understanding why you want to achieve something and being committed to it may not be enough.

Conversely, maybe you have the belief and commitment to reach your desired state but not really grasp or understand why you want to achieve it, so it's all a bit meaningless. Again, you are unlikely to achieve it.

Or, if you aren't committed or don't know what your desired state is, you end up drifting through life.

Figure 6: The three requirements to move from Present to Desired state

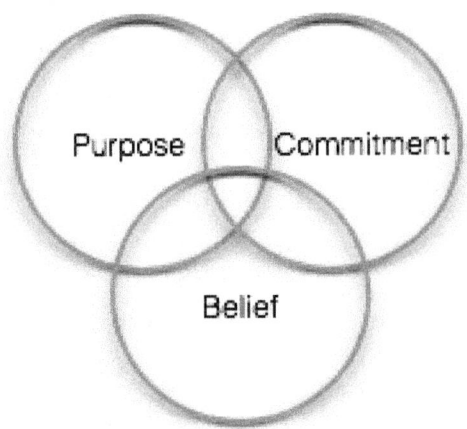

Here are some suggestions:

- Work with a colleague, friend, or coach and brainstorm both states: present state and desired state.
- When you have a clear idea about your desired state, ask yourself, 'How will I know when I have achieved that?'

My questions are:

- Where are you today at this present moment?
- Where do you want to be?
- What is your desired state?
- Finally, what is preventing you from reaching it?

For what purpose?

Developing a meaning for what we want to achieve

Now that you have considered where you want to get to, or what you want to achieve, do you really know why?

Have you paused to consider the purpose behind wanting that?

How often have you wanted to obtain or achieve something, and then achieved it only to discover it wasn't really what you wanted? Sometimes we may want something, but when it happens it doesn't give us the feelings, or the satisfaction, or the happiness we had been hoping for.

A simple, and often profound, exercise is to dig a little deeper into why you want to obtain, achieve, or do something. Spend some time to really develop an understanding of 'why'.

When I'm working with clients this is generally where I start. They say 'my goal is to do this' or 'have this'. I start asking why they want that and keep drilling down until they have hit the core of why they want it.

Sometimes this is easy, and sometimes it's hard.

Instead of actually using the word 'why', the question I ask is: 'for what purpose...?' This encourages the person being questioned to start her answer with 'so that...'

I don't use 'why' often, as when people are asked this they often start answering by saying 'because...'. This creates a blame type answer, or an answer that is embedded in the past. For example, I may ask you, 'Why do you want a pay rise?' You may say, 'because I have been in this role for three years and I think I deserve it.' On the other hand, I could ask *'For what purpose* do you want a pay rise?' You may say, *'so that* I feel I am rewarded fairly for the work I do.'

Sometimes when I say, 'it's a woman's prerogative to rule the world', people ask me why.

If I start with 'because', I am going to blame something from the past. *'Because* I feel women have not been treated fairly in the corporate environment.'

If the question is changed to *'For what purpose* is it a woman's prerogative to rule the world?' I can start by saying, *'so that* we have a diversity of gender, culture, age, or disability.'

I keep drilling down on each new answer.

'So that we have more diversity of thought.'

'So that there is a diversity in energy in workplaces.'

'So that our vibrational levels operate at higher levels for the good of all.'

This is my perspective, although asking myself these questions is probably the first time I have thought deeply about the purpose behind why I love working with women to help them to move into more senior leadership roles!

It's like seeing the lights come on – something suddenly becomes clear.

If a woman is looking to be promoted, understanding the 'why' and the deep reasons for wanting a promotion can create a clear direction to achieve that.

Often people say they want something without understanding the deep reason for wanting that. Learning what those deep reasons are can often create the urgency and commitment to achieve it, uncover a new direction to achieve it, or help them realise that it *isn't* actually something they necessarily want.

I once spent an hour with a client, Jane, just asking her the purpose behind her goal. I kept taking her up a layer at a time to really understand her deeper and higher purpose.

While Jane initially found it frustrating to keep answering the same question, she became speechless when she realised her goal was driven by a sense of guilt for something that had happened in her life previously – her future focus had been to alleviate that guilt. Once she realised that, her goal didn't change, but it meant she could release that guilt and focus on where she wanted to get to.

Here's an example of how you can ask '*for what purpose* …?'

> Mary has identified that she wants to be more confident in meetings.
>
> I ask, '*For what purpose* do you want to be confident in meetings?'
>
> She replies, '*So that* I am confident that I can ask questions if I need to or make a point about something.'
>
> I ask, '*For what purpose* do you want to be able to ask questions or make a point about something?'

She replies, '*So that* I feel I fully understand what is going on and can contribute meaningfully to the meeting.'

I ask, '*For what purpose* do you want to fully understand and contribute?'

She replies, '*So that* I feel valued in my role and sought after for my knowledge.'

I ask, '*For what purpose* do you want to feel valued and sought after for your knowledge?'

She replies, '*So that* I am fully contributing and offering expertise that is of value to my team.'

So Mary wants to feel more confident in meetings so she can contribute and fully step into her role and provide the expertise the team needs.

Then I could ask, 'What prevents you from feeling confident in meetings now?' Or 'What would you need to do to feel valued and sought after in your role?'

Here are some suggestions:

- Practise asking yourself the purpose for wanting something. Start your answer with 'so that…'
- Ask someone else if you can practise this with them. Again, explain that the answer should start with 'so that…'

My questions are:

- Take your desired state from the previous section and ask yourself, 'For what purpose do I want to achieve that?'
  Take that answer and ask the question again.
  Then take that answer and ask the question again.
  Keep asking for four or five times. Make sure you start each answer with 'so that…'.
- When you feel you are clear about why you want to achieve your desired state, check again – do you know the deeper purpose behind that?
- If you don't know, what do you need to do to find out?

Coding your internal and external experiences

You have now spent some time thinking about where you are and where you want to get to (Present to Desired state). You have also considered the purpose behind wanting to achieve that – the 'why'.

To really achieve something, it has to come from within you. You have to see it, hear it, feel it and maybe even taste and smell it. Before reaching your desired state, you have to represent the experience as if you have already achieved it.

In Neuro-Linguistic Programming (NLP), this internal representation is called a 4-tuple – and it is a way of codifying our experience.

4-tuple is the inner experience we have at any given moment, which relates to five categories of sensory experience: the visual sense (V – seeing), the auditory sense (A – hearing), the kinaesthetic sense (K – feeling), and the olfactory (O – smelling) and gustatory (G – tasting) senses. In NLP, these senses are known as representational systems – how we represent our memories and experiences back to ourselves. Often we are not aware of these consciously unless they are brought to our attention.

I am going to say one word to you. Lock in the first thoughts that come to mind when you see the word on the page.

That word is 'circus'.

What first came to mind? Was it a picture of something – a circus tent, or an elephant, or maybe a ringmaster inside a tent? Was it the word 'circus' inside your mind? Did you feel anything when you saw the word 'circus'? Excitement?

If I ask a group to do this activity, everyone in the group will have a different experience – they have re-presented the word back and coded it as a picture, a sound, a smell, a taste, a feeling, or a combination of these. Each person will say something different.

We take in external information from around us using our five senses, then these five senses are used internally to process and store this information. We can internally see pictures, hear sounds, feel feelings, and even smell and taste. These ongoing experiences can be coded as a combination of these sensory classes and represent our inner experience at a given moment in time.

We can use this process to describe our ongoing experiences. As you are reading, imagine that you are describing the experience to me.

> Auditory: Listen to your internal dialogue. What are the words you are saying to yourself as you are reading? What is the tone and pace of your voice?
>
> Visual: What are you seeing? How are the words appearing as you read? What internal pictures are you making?
>
> Kinaesthetic: What are you feeling? Maybe the weight of the book or reading device, the chair you are sitting on, and the warm or cool temperature of where you are sitting?
>
> Olfactory: What are you smelling? Maybe some food cooking, coffee or tea, or some flowers in the room?
>
> Gustatory: What are you tasting? What is coming to your awareness about your sense of taste?

As you become aware of how you are codifying your experiences, your awareness of how you 'do' the world will grow. As your awareness grows, so do your choices in life. By changing some of these sensory experiences (or not), your experience or memory of the experience can change.

When I work with someone who has identified a goal they want to achieve, I want them to code it internally through their senses. Our brain cannot differentiate fact from fiction. Therefore, creating the experience of something before it occurs allows the brain to code it as fact, as if it has already occurred.

Imagine that you want to have an attribute or strength that you have observed in others, or have experienced yourself in the past. How these are codified can be replicated, so that you can recreate them for yourself as if you are having that experience now.

I will explain further how you can use the 4-tuple when I describe how you can change your goals into well-formed outcomes.

Here are some suggestions:

- Practise noticing what you notice about your experiences. Become aware of your internal dialogue, the pictures you are making, and the feelings you experience.
- Ask someone else what they first notice when you say the word 'circus'.

My questions are:

- How are you representing the experience that you want to achieve? Can you see it, hear it, feel it, and maybe even taste and smell it?

- Think about a memory you have and notice what you notice about that. Are there pictures in your mind, an internal dialogue, or feelings you experience when you remember that memory?

Those limiting thoughts you may have[1]

You may understand 'why' (your purpose) you want to achieve something, but if your commitment to achieve it is low, so is the likelihood of success. Your commitment can be impacted by your beliefs – do you believe you can achieve it?

When you are focusing on where you are presently and where you want to get to (P to D), and you have created a 4-tuple to internalise and code the desired state from a sensory perspective, you may find that there are still a number of limiting factors or beliefs preventing you from achieving that desired state.

It's been said that whatever you believe becomes your reality. You do not believe what you see; rather, you see what you already believe. For this reason, two people facing the same situation may interpret it differently, act according to their different beliefs, and experience different outcomes.

Our beliefs are assumptions we have about the world. They grow from what we see, hear, experience, read, or think about. They also grow from what we absorb from our parents, our family, our culture, and our childhood experiences. They are built as we go along so we tend not to question them. Once a belief is formed, you will work overtime to prove it right, even if the belief is something negative like 'nobody likes me' or 'I am a failure'. But beliefs can change.

In NLP, beliefs fall into one of two overarching categories: empowering

---

[1] Reference: Dilts, R. (1990). Changing Belief Systems with NLP, Meta Publications

or limiting. Empowering beliefs help us confidently make changes and decisions. Limiting beliefs do the exact opposite, and can prevent us from changing or trying something new and diminish our energy. Limiting beliefs typically sound like 'I am ugly', 'I will never be successful', or 'I can't work with those kind of people'. They are usually outside of our conscious awareness, meaning we don't even know that they exist.

It is only by identifying and understanding your beliefs, which are at the core of who you are, that you can use them, or change them, to guide your decisions and behaviour in all areas of life. This in turn builds your commitment to achieving something.

Your beliefs govern you, even if they are harmful. The more understanding and control we have over our beliefs, the more choice we present to ourselves. Admit and nurture only those thoughts that enhance your positive programming and move you towards your goals.

Sometimes a belief may have been useful as a child, such as the belief instilled in many of us to 'not talk to strangers'. However, this isn't a useful belief as we grow up and have a need to build new connections (either for work or for relationships) with people we don't know. This belief doesn't serve us beyond a certain point in time and may become a limiting belief. Limiting beliefs can also be based on assumptions that are not true. For instance, some of us may say 'I can't draw' or 'I'm not creative', which becomes true because we believe it.

Beliefs can be a result of significant experiences in our lives. A wonderful belief I formed at a young age (around ten years old) was that I was an awesome swimmer, as I had won the swimming championship for my primary school region for three years running. The following year this belief was completely busted when I moved to a much larger high school and competed with a much larger group. I found that actually I was an average swimmer, and struggled to even get a place in the races I competed in!

The reason I focus on people's limiting beliefs is to help them to understand that they can change how they 'do' the world. Having someone becoming aware of what beliefs are limiting them or preventing them from achieving their desired state is often all that is needed to move on and achieve it.

When attempting to overcome limiting beliefs, the first step is to become aware of them. With my swimming I didn't consciously make a decision to not try so hard after the first year in high school. However, I developed a limiting belief from that point on as I unconsciously believed I couldn't compete against town kids who had access to swimming pools every day when I didn't. It was only many years later that I understood why I had given up on my dream to be a champion swimmer.

Our limiting beliefs have a way of hiding from us, though you may be aware of other people's limiting beliefs due to the way they may say things. For example:

- 'My goal cannot be achieved.'
- 'My goal could be achieved, but I don't have the ability to do it.'
- 'I don't deserve this because of [something I am or am not or something I have or have not done]."

Think about the way you say things to yourself or others. If you find yourself saying things like this you need to ask yourself:

- Why is this goal unattainable?

- What skills do I need to develop to achieve this goal?
- Why don't I deserve to achieve this goal?

Continue to uncover the limiting beliefs that stand in the way of achieving your goal – you may find that one limiting belief leads to another, and then another. Keep digging and questioning to uncover those limiting beliefs that are preventing you from achieving your goals. These limiting beliefs affect your behaviour, but once identified and dealt with they will start to lose their power over you.

Limiting beliefs have formed for a reason, which was generally in your best interests at the time of forming. Think about the reasons behind some of your beliefs. Simply thinking about why you believe something is sometimes enough to see how limiting or ridiculous the belief is.

Sometimes evidence that we can do something is all that is needed to change a limiting belief. Just try doing it. Once proven wrong, the belief will change instantly and lose its power.

Here are some suggestions:

- When you focus on your desired state (the end goal), think about anything that may be preventing you from getting there.
- Think back to major events from your past and consider what beliefs may have formed from that time.

My questions are:

- What is preventing you from achieving your desired state?
- Where do you think your limiting beliefs stem from?

- Consider one of your limiting beliefs. What would you need to do to remove or diminish this limiting belief and create a more empowering one?
- What are some empowering beliefs that will help you reach your desired outcome?

Just keep on going and keep believing in your own original vision, no matter what odds you have to overcome. And especially don't be stopped by your own fears.

—Angelina Maccarone

Our values

Values are a set of standards that determine our attitudes, choices and actions. They are like a compass that guides our lives, often functioning at an unconscious level, but guiding us nonetheless.

We all have an internalised system of values that we have developed throughout our lives – some that we may have developed independently, and some that we have inherited or absorbed from our families and culture.

Values are principles or qualities that we consider important, such as honesty, education, or hard work. Our individual values affect us at the deepest level. Every decision we make is based on our values, which we use as a guide to either avoid or aspire to something.

Understanding your value priorities can help lay important groundwork for making sound career decisions that fit your unique pattern of values, interests and talents. Work-related values underlie our choices about work. Some people value creativity; others place a premium on income or contribution.

Values are who we are. When we honour our values we find life is fulfilling, and feels like it's in flow. When we don't honour our values, we can feel anxious. For example, if you value integrity and you are asked to cover up for a colleague at work, this will cause stress. You may not consciously be aware that it goes against one of your values, but you will sense the discomfort.

The following quote from *The Co-active Coaching Book* by Whitworth, Kinsey-House, and Sandahl summarises values thus:

Values are intangible. They are not something we do or have. Money, for example is not a value, although the things you might do with money could be considered values: fun; creativity; peace of mind; service to others. Travel is not a value. Gardening is not a value. But both are examples of cherished activities that honour certain values such as: adventure; learning; nature; spirituality.

A value is who you 'are', not what you would like to be. A value is internal, something that resonates with you.

Sometimes you may feel tempted to pick values you think you 'ought' to have. Make sure you take the time to understand which values truly resonate with you.

Workplaces are becoming more collaborative and people are increasingly looking not just for jobs, but also for organisations whose values and culture align with their own. By the same token, the most effective organisations attract people who already share most of their key values.

Identifying your values

When you understand your values, real change can occur. We all have more than one core value in our life. The following exercise will help you discover the hierarchy of importance of the different values you hold.

1) Start by asking the question, 'What is important in my life?' Then continue asking, 'What else is important in my life?' Underline those that are most important. Use the words on page 79 to help you.

2) Now narrow down the list and circle the top eight values that are absolutely essential to satisfy you in your work and life.

3) Chunk words or clarify meaning for yourself, as some values may be similar.

4) After you have elicited a set of eight values, rank them by asking, 'Is 1 more important than 2?' 'Is 1 more important than 3?', and so on. Put a mark against the value that is most important.

5) Now write out the top values and define what they mean to you.

To help you with this, think about your key life decisions. It could be when you changed jobs, moved house, or started or left a relationship.

In reflecting on these key moments, consider which values were being either honoured or not at that point. Consider the values that fuelled the decision-making.

You may be surprised when you compare your values this way. Values you may have thought were very important might be further down your hierarchy than you first realised.

Fairness	Flexibility	Teamwork	Integrity
Competence	Surroundings	Leading	Prestige
Mastery	Time freedom	Caring	Achievement
Risk	Security	Competition	Respect
Leading edge	High earnings	Cooperation	Responsibility
Detail oriented	Action oriented	Diversity	Power
Social activism	Structure	Collaboration	Influence
Learning	Relaxed pace	Humour	Appreciation
Excellence	Casual	Harmony	Helping
Focus	Quiet	Autonomy	Belonging
Creativity	Organised	Recognition	Community
Variety	Excitement	Support	Equality
Growth	Pressure	Trust	Independence
Knowledge	Predictability	People contact	Contributing
Control	Location	Independence	Service
Adventure	Public contact	Fun	Authenticity
Helping	Status	Balance	Commitment
Initiating	Honesty	Having impact	Balance
Cultural identity	Meeting deadlines	Open communication	Comfortable income

Some other useful questions to help clarify your values:

- What must you have in your life to feel fulfilled?
- What are the values you absolutely must honour – or a part of you dies?
- What values do you see in your own life?
- What values do you sell out on first?
- Where do your values show up?

- Which values are sometimes neglected?
- Where are you too flexible?
- What value is being stretched a bit too much?
- What are your wants versus your musts?
- Where are you an automatic yes or no?
- Where do you limit yourself?
- If you didn't limit yourself, what might you do?
- What value would that uphold?
- Where are you too comfortable?
- What are you willing to risk?
- What will free you up?

Being comfortable with change

There are plenty of people in this world who give up when the going gets a little tough. There is plenty in life that can prevent you from achieving what you want to achieve and reaching that 'desired state'.

This is about

- Being satisfied with where you are in your life
- Looking in the mirror and comfortable with what you see
- Being resilient enough to face what life throws at you
- Having choice.

You will remember in the introduction to this book I mentioned that early in my career I took no initiative in shaping my future. I felt like my life was being shaped by external events and people, rather than by me. I came to the realisation that my career choices (or lack thereof) were harming my strengths, skills, and happiness. I needed to be able to move out of my comfort zone and face my fears to start focusing on my strengths and what I loved to do. I also needed to stop blaming other people, things, and circumstances for where I was in life.

First though, I had to work out what I wanted to change and what I wanted to do.

The steps I followed are pretty basic and I know they work. This is about creating more choice in your life.

Step 1: Figure out what you want.

Step 2: Be aware of your own responses to change.

Step 3: Choose how you respond.

Step 1. What do you want to achieve (desired state)?

You are well on the way to working out your desired state, if you haven't already. You understand where you are currently (present state), you have created a sensory-specific experience for what you want (4-tuple), you have worked on your beliefs and have a better understanding of your limiting beliefs, and you have identified your most important values.

It's like driving a car.

When you learnt to drive, at first it took a lot of time and effort. It felt like you were paying attention to every single little detail, aware of everything going on around you. You probably felt overwhelmed and exhausted after every drive. But as you became accustomed to driving it became easier and required less conscious awareness. Now, you drive without even thinking and manage to safely get where you want to go without having to work too hard. You remember the awkwardness of those initial steps, but now you 'know' how to drive you don't give it a second thought.

Just like driving a car, working on your awareness, your beliefs and your values will become easier and easier the more you practise, and your future direction will become clear.

Step 2. Be aware of your responses to change

Have you thought about your comfort zone? Can you recall a time when you were out of your comfort zone? How did you feel?

- Anxious?
- Uncomfortable?
- Afraid?
- Out of control?
- Frustrated?
- Excited?

What did you do?

Most people are very familiar with their comfort zone. As human beings we crave certainty and try to stay in our comfort zone at any cost. We can go through life denying that we have to do something, blaming someone or something else, and justifying our actions. This makes us a victim of external forces and means we will *never* move out of our comfort zone.

When we are in our comfort zone we are doing the 'same old' stuff. We know the people we work with, we may have had the same desk for some time, we are familiar with our surroundings, the work we do is pretty much the same day to day, and we are not learning anything new.

When you are out of your comfort zone how do you respond? You may experience physical responses such as increased heart rate, sweaty palms, or a knot in the pit of your stomach. We perceive these as negative – to be avoided.

Think back again to the first time you drove a car. Did you experience any of these physical reactions? You may have been very anxious. With time, you probably overcame those feelings and can now drive calmly, effortlessly, and skilfully without even thinking.

This is evidence that being outside the comfort zone has some relationship to learning new things. By definition, the comfort zone consists of things you know – which means you can't learn something new from within the comfort zone. The zone outside of the comfort zone is called the 'learning zone'.

How much you want something, or want to change something, will have a direct relationship to your willingness to feel the 'pain' of the learning zone and stay with it until it becomes comfortable and familiar.

Moving out your comfort zone can feel like jumping out of a plane and hoping your parachute works.

Figure 8: Comfort Zone / Learning Zone

For one of my clients, Mel, it was a matter of encouraging her to start dipping her toe into the water, to move her into her learning zone in small steps. She had a great deal of trouble confronting staff and avoided it at all costs. She would go through a complex series of justifications as to why she couldn't confront team members. Naturally this was having a major impact on the team.

Most of us crave certainty. We like the same old stuff, and we like to know what to expect at any time with no surprises. We like our comfort zone. However, if we never leave our comfort zone we can't learn and grow, and we will become bored and complacent.

The more we do something we are *uncomfortable* about, the more *comfortable* we become, and the bigger our comfort zone becomes.

Do you know anyone who stays in their comfort zone? When a new idea is suggested or they are asked to do something different, they may respond with things like:

- 'That would never work.'
- 'That's not how it's done.'
- 'I could never do that.'
- 'I haven't been trained to do that.'
- 'It's not in my job description.'
- 'My family didn't believe in that.'
- 'I'm just a…'
- 'It's because I'm too young.'
- 'It's because I'm too old.'
- 'You can't teach an old dog new tricks.'

One of my favourite things to do is help people develop their public speaking skills. I see people implement these types of excuses over and over again to avoid trying. This perhaps isn't surprising when you consider that the fear of speaking in public is often rated ahead of the fear of dying.

We refer to these strategies of avoidance as the '**DBJ**':

- Deny
- Blame
- Justify

Others avoidance strategies I hear are:

- 'I don't need to know how to do that.' (denying the need to learn)
- 'I can't lose weight because I have a slow metabolism.' (blaming your metabolism)
- 'My manager made me…' (blaming your manager)
- 'This isn't part of my job description.' (justifying why you can't do something)
- 'I'm late because …' (justifying why you're late)

Lateness is a classic. 'I'm late because of the traffic.' 'I'm late because of the trains.' I understand that you can't control the traffic and you can't control the trains. The question is, what can you control? You can change the time you leave, listen to traffic reports, or find other ways to travel. All these things are under your control.

Once you start picking yourself up on this you'll find that you run out of excuses, which previously might have prevented you from doing things.

Now think of something you have always wanted to do. What are your DBJs? They might include 'I don't have time', 'I can't afford it', 'I'm not skilled enough to do it', 'my family wouldn't approve', or 'I don't really want to do that anyway'.

When you are DBJing you are being a *victim*.

Step 3. Choose how you respond

Here comes one of the simplest ways to shift our mindset from being stuck or a victim to exploring possibilities and becoming master of our own destiny.

When you catch yourself in a **Deny**, the best response is to add 'yet' or 'at this point in time' to your statement. For example, 'I'm not skilled enough to do it *yet*.' 'I could never do that *at this point in time*.'

When you catch yourself in a **Blame**, the best response is to ask yourself, 'What is my 50%?' In any interaction or situation you are involved in, you contribute at least 50% to the outcome. For example, during an argument with someone it's easy to blame the other person for being bad tempered or mean. The question is, 'How did you contribute to the upset – what was your 50%?'

When you catch yourself in a **Justify**, it is also useful to consider your 50%. In the example 'I'm late because of the traffic', it's easy to justify why you were late – the road conditions, other drivers, poor city planning, traffic lights... and so on. The question is what percentage you want to give to these. This is not about traffic, it's about you being late and your part in that. What is your 50%?

Instead of denying that you can achieve something, *accept* your own actions.

Instead of blaming something or someone, *take responsibility* for your own actions.

Instead of justifying why you did or didn't do something, *be accountable* for your actions.

Ask yourself the question, 'What if the opposite were true?' In the example 'this isn't part of my job description', ask yourself 'what if the opposite was true and this *was* part of my job description?' It doesn't change the facts; however it does create a shift in your mindset and open up different possibilities.

This is often enough to shift your perspective and create some change in what you are or are not doing.

Once Mel starting taking action, stopped justifying her staff's actions, and actually confronted them (in rapport) about their behaviour, things started to change. While it is unlikely that all the team members will ever really like each other, this simple change has been enough to create a degree of respect and cooperation between team members. And now Mel is aware of the importance of moving out of her comfort zone to effect action.

I had another big 'aha' moment about how great these techniques are when I was contacted by another client, Susan, who wanted to achieve some big goals but kept finding that they just weren't happening for one reason or another.

As I mentioned earlier, as human beings we crave certainty and will try to stay in our comfort zone at any cost.

Susan was a victim. There were lots of reasons why she wasn't achieving her goals: her husband didn't support her with achieving them, the timing wasn't right, it was too soon after Christmas, it was too close to Easter, it was winter, it was summer… on and on it went.

Do you know people like that?

Susan needed to move from the Deny, Blame, Justify strategy to the Acceptance, Responsibility, Accountability strategy. To accept that it was up to her and stop denying it; to take responsibility for her own actions and stop blaming others; and to become accountable for her own action (or inaction). She had to move from being a victim to being a learner by stepping into her learning zone.

And she did. It was confronting and difficult for her, but she started facing her excuses, inaction, and victim strategies and owned the actions required to change. She allowed herself to be uncomfortable: out of her comfort zone.

Some suggestions are:

- Get out of your comfort zone.
- Stop DBJing.
- **Accept** that it's up to you, become **Responsible** for your own actions and become **Accountable** for your life.

My questions are:

- What if the opposite were true (to what you currently believe)?
- How is staying in your comfort zone preventing you from achieving something amazing?

Excuses change nothing, but make everyone feel better.

—Mason Cooley

Creating a well formed outcome (putting it all together)

The 'D' in Present State to Desired State represents the end point: where you want to get to. Often when I ask a client what their D is, they describe something intangible or wishy-washy.

If you create goals for yourself on a regular basis, do you find that you often don't achieve them? One reason may be that your goals are externally focused – something you want to do, have, or be. For example, if you say, 'I want to be a senior manager', you are referring to a position that you are trying to attain, which is outside of you and who you currently are.

Taking something external – a goal – and turning it into something internal creates a far more compelling way of achieving it.

Creating an internal Desired State is about creating, in NLP terms, a *well-formed outcome*.

A well-formed outcome is like an opening gambit in chess. It sets the scene for the rest of the game. A well-formed outcome makes the difference between wanting something in theory, and becoming able to get it in practice.[2]

Any goal, big or small, can be turned into a well-formed outcome. If several steps are needed for you to move from your present state to your desired state, you can use well-formed outcomes for every step towards

---

[2] Collingwood, C., & Collingwood, J. (2001). *The NLP Field Guide, Part 1: A Reference Manual of Practitioner Level Patterns*, Emergent Publications, Sydney.

achieving your end state.

It's ultimately up to you and no-one else to create and achieve your own your well-formed outcome. A coach, mentor, friend, or colleague can help you through the process, but you have to do the work.

Use the KIS principle – Keep It Simple – when planning steps towards your well-formed outcome. The smaller and more practical the steps, the more likely that you will achieve them.

The questions below form the basis for creating a well-formed outcome. Much of the work has been completed already with the sections already covered in this chapter, but this is where we pull it all together.

A well-formed outcome should be tangible and sensory specific.

1) What do you want to achieve? This must be stated in the positive (what you do want, not what you don't want).

2) Is it achievable? Has this ever been done before?

3) Is achieving this outcome under your control? The outcome must be able to be self-initiated and self-maintained (i.e., you don't need other people to help you achieve it).

4) 4-tuple – you will remember this from earlier in this chapter. Use sensory language to describe experiencing the achievement of this goal, which you can accept as evidence that you have achieved it.

   a. What do you see? Close your eyes and imagine that the outcome has been reached. What are you seeing around you, what are you doing, and what are other people doing?

   b. What can you hear? What are other people saying and what are you saying to yourself?

   c. What are you feeling?

   d. What can you taste or smell?

5) For what purpose do you want to achieve this outcome? You should already have completed this step at the beginning of this chapter. Start your answer with '*so that…*' Keep repeating this question until you really reach the highest and best purpose for achieving this goal.

6) Is the goal ecological? This means that its achievement will do no harm to yourself, others, or the environment. Are all the costs and consequences of achieving your outcome, including the time involved, acceptable to you and anyone else affected by it? For example, will there be any issues with friends' expectations of the way you were, compared to how you will be when you achieve this? And if you could have this outcome now, would you take it?.

7) What resources do you need to achieve this – tangible and intangible?

8) What is the first step in achieving this goal? Is the first step achievable? What's the first thing you can do?

Some people may experience rising feelings of anxiety when completing this sort of exercise. Face this feeling and identify its cause.

This is a structured way to define where you are currently and where you want to get to, and to quiet down that voice inside that may be expressing your deepest concerns and fears.

Having a tangible first step to achieving a goal and acting on it will usually start the process going.

Once you have identified and achieved that first step, what's the next step?

When you have achieved the next step, what's the step after that? And so on.

A suggestion:

- Work through this process and create a well-formed outcome for yourself. Start with something simple that you want to achieve in the short term.

My questions are:

- What has this experience been like?
- When you worked through the process above did you feel excited, or a little perturbed?
- Check in. Now that you have completed this exercise, are you surprised by anything? Did you have some 'aha' moments? Did you experience any feelings of anxiety?

It still takes work though

Everything is almost in place to reach that outcome you have identified. By creating a well-formed outcome, you have internalised what it is you want to achieve. It's no longer something outside of you that you are waiting to happen. This outcome is part of you. You cannot not achieve this now!

But you still have to work and put in the effort required to achieve this – it doesn't just happen.

This section will provide you with some ways to speed your results along.

Have you ever been studying or trying to work something out so intensely that your head hurts? I'm not necessarily talking about having a headache; I'm talking about those times when your head just seems too full and you cannot fit one more thing into it.

I remember many years ago participating in a two-day strategic planning session for a primary school council. We were mapping out the school's five-year plan. By the middle of the first afternoon I felt like banging my head on the table to try to fit more in. My head just seemed too full and was hurting from the lack of space.

Feelings like this actually result from too much disjointed information. I didn't have a logical way to file it away while trying to retrieve other information. If only I knew then what I know now about releasing that tension in a way that fosters creative thinking.

What I'm about to describe is like decluttering your wardrobe and freeing up space within it. It's called *creating a high-performance mind*.

Developing a high-performance mind gives you the ability to 'be present'.

Being in the moment, aware and present, is difficult. So often we are thinking about what happened in the past, or what is going to happen in the future. Developing the strength to be present and in the moment takes practice.

I suggest you incorporate two activities into your daily routine: an aerobic activity and some structured meditation.

Alphabet Charts[3]

I previously mentioned our conscious and unconscious processes. This is an exercise for experiencing the interface between these processes, which can be useful in many situations to help 'reboot' the brain. The level of difficulty can be adjusted to suit different people's experience and involves a drill that splits our attention.

I often use this exercise as an after-lunch activity in an all-day training session, as it creates a break between intense periods of work or learning activity to facilitate integration, and also creates mental alertness in that after-lunch lull.

This exercise allows you to change in state from concentration to creativity, allowing different resources to emerge.

Do it often enough and you will learn to split your attention two ways simultaneously and, with practice, more than two ways. It allows for creative thinking and different perspectives to emerge, and oxygenates the body and brain through physical activity.

The alphabet chart can also be used to break out of a strongly unresourceful or overwhelmed state. During my moment of feeling overwhelmed during the school council strategy session, I could certainly have used this exercise to create a more resourceful and useful state to

---

[3] Developed by John Grinder and Judith DeLozier. Adapted from Collingwood, C., & Collingwood, J. (2001). *The NLP Field Guide, Part 1: A Reference Manual of Practitioner Level Patterns*, Emergent Publications, Sydney.

continue functioning to the end of that day's session.

Creating an Alphabet Chart

(See sample chart below.)

1. Write the alphabet in conventional order, on flip chart paper, in five or six lines of letters. Leave sufficient space below each line to write another line of letters.
2. Below the letter L in the alphabet, in a different colour and the same size, write R or T, below the letter R, write L or T, below the letter T, write R or L
3. Below each remaining letter of the alphabet write the letter L, R, or T in the same size as the alphabet. You may have up to two of any L, R, or T next to each other
4. When your alphabet chart becomes familiar, write a new one with different combinations of L, R, and T below the alphabet, still ensuring that the letters below L, R, and T in the alphabet are different.

L stands for 'left', R stands for 'right', and T stands for 'together'.

Using the Alphabet Chart

When you first use alphabet charts it is helpful to have a partner or coach beside you. They watch you complete the exercise while keeping an eye on the chart to ensure that you are completing the correct sequence.

- Stand in front of the chart so both you and your coach can see the whole chart.
- Read out the letters of the alphabet in a steady rhythm while simultaneously raising your right arm when you see 'R' below the letter you are reading, your left arm when you see 'L', and both arms together when you see 'T'. Proceed through the chart from start to finish unless you make a mistake.
- If your coach notices that you have made a mistake, they will ask you to stop, shake off your present state, relax your body, and start again from the beginning.
- Once you have made it through the entire chart, at the same pace and with no mistakes, make it a bit more challenging by speeding up your pace. Ideally, you should just be able to get through the chart without error.
- When you want a greater stretch, raise the opposite leg at the same time as the left or right arm, and bounce or dip both knees for T.
- To limit excessive familiarity with your chart, read it in different directions. Start from the end and work backwards, start at the right hand end of each line and work backwards, start at the top right and work to the bottom left, and so on.
- Make a new chart with different combinations of L, R, and T. Once you are familiar with the process, go ahead and try them out on your own.

Spend as long as you can completing this activity. You will find after a while that your body will start to buzz and hum and you will feel invigorated. Fifteen minutes a day is a wonderful investment of your time to create a high-performance mind.

Sample Alphabet Chart

A	B	C	D	E	F
L	T	R	R	L	R
G	H	I	J	K	L
T	L	R	R	T	R
M	N	O	P	Q	R
L	R	L	T	T	L
S	T	U	V	X	Y
T	R	L	L	R	T

Meditation

Corporations can tend to shy away from 'weird' stuff that is a bit out there. This was certainly the case when I first experienced a cultural change program within a major financial institution. We were required to sit in a large group, close our eyes, focus our breathing, and follow the guided instructions. It wasn't called 'meditating', it was called 'creating a high-performance mind' – so that the group would feel comfortable trying it.

That was many years ago; now it is much more common to hear about executives who regularly meditate and practise yoga.

It really does still the mind, allowing creative thoughts to bubble up, and gives us the ability to control our brainwaves. A meditative mind is one that can enter, at will, the state of consciousness that is most beneficial and desirable for any circumstance.

Have you ever sat in a meeting and suddenly had one of those 'aha' moments when everything comes together? Maybe you have had a sense of being in a different space – the way you think and feel changes – as you 'get it'? This can happen at unlikely times: in the shower, out walking or running, or driving the car. In these situations, the way your brain works literally changes: if you were connected to an electroencephalograph (EEG) machine, it would show the changes in your brainwaves.

There are four brainwave patterns:

Beta

This brainwave pattern is the fastest and predominates in the normal waking day. It is necessary for logical thinking, problem solving and managing normal daily activities.

If beta waves go into overdrive, you may experience panic. Your head is full of thoughts competing for your attention. It's hard to focus. You can't think straight. Too much beta, even if it falls short of panic, causes stress. Most business people could benefit from keeping their beta waves under better control.

Alpha

When alpha brainwaves predominate, you feel dreamy, relaxed, and detached. Your mind visualises things that seem real and you are so absorbed in your daydream that reality does not even enter your consciousness. A predominance of alpha waves can make you experience life as a kind of fantasy.

Alpha brainwaves are important because they form the gateway between your conscious and unconscious mind. In the absence of alpha waves, you will not remember your dreams when you wake after sleep – even if you know you were dreaming vividly. Alpha waves can help you bring that great idea that has been sitting in the back of your mind to the surface.

Theta

Theta waves are our unconscious brainwaves; responsible for memories, sensations, emotions, creativity, and inspiration. These waves are prevalent during so-called peak experiences of creativity and insight.

While theta waves are associated with creativity, they must work with other brainwaves to bring the idea, knowledge or insight into your conscious mind. When you get the feeling that the answer is on the tip of your tongue, or a creative insight just happens, then your theta waves are working. Most people do not know how to tap into the richness of these waves at will.

Delta

Delta brainwaves are the lowest frequency, deepest waves of the unconscious mind. They continue even when everything else has closed down, particularly during deep sleep.

Delta waves give you intuition and empathy – a 'sixth sense'. They help you keep in touch with your deepest knowledge, the things you know without knowing. People who experience strong delta waves often 'gut feelings' that may often prove right.

Figure 8: Brainwave frequencies

Frequency (megahertz)
- 38
  - Beta (multi-tasking, logical thinking)
- 14
  - Alpha (relaxed, single point of focus)

Alpha Bridge

- 8
  - Theta (creativity, emotions and memories)
- 4
  - Delta (intuition, empathy)
- 0.5

Our state of consciousness is made up of an ever-changing combination of the four types of brainwaves, and none is any 'better' than the others –

though some combinations may be more appropriate for certain situations.

For creative problem solving, we need a pattern referred to as the 'Awakened Mind' – which is a combination of all four types simultaneously. It is in this state that you experience 'aha!' moments – creative insights into problems or possibilities.

It is possible to develop the ability to control your brainwaves: to induce the state of consciousness you desire; to become calm when you are stressed; to foster the 'awakened mind' at will.

Meditation is an important tool to do this.

Mastering brainwaves is necessary to enable a high-performance mind. A high-performance mind is one that can enter at will the state of consciousness that is most beneficial and most desirable for any circumstance.

This is a very powerful method, though to be effective it should be practised daily. It is also a great way to get to sleep at night. In some cases it can even reduce the amount of sleep people require. It may help to make a recording of the instructions to use the first few times, as you will need to have your eyes closed.

Method of meditation to create a high-performance mind

(20 minutes)

Sit comfortably.

Close your eyes for 30 seconds. (Your brainwaves will drop to low beta.)

Open your eyes. (Your brainwaves will come up two cycles.)

Close your eyes 30 seconds. (Your brainwaves will drop to low alpha.)

Open your eyes for five seconds. (This will pull you up to the threshold of the alpha bridge.)

Close your eyes. (You will immediately jump over the alpha bridge into theta.)

Turn your attention inward – to yourself.

Place your focus on your breathing – breathe easily and deeply.

Breathe and relax into your body.

Breathe away any tension.

Place your focus on your forehead and allow your muscles to relax.

Now move your focus to around your eyes and behind the eyes – let the muscles relax.

Move your focus to your cheeks and relax your jaw.

Relax the muscles on your tongue and now around your lips.

Now place your focus on your neck.

Send messages of relaxation across your shoulders and allow it to flow down both arms, all the way to your fingertips.

Now place your focus on your spine and back, allowing the relaxation to flow through.

And allow it to go deep to your stomach, to the very centre of your body.

Move your focus to your hips and pelvis.

Relax your legs – your knees, and down to your calves, your ankles, and your feet.

Focus your breathing – the breath in and out.

Breathe easily and deeply.

Now very gently, in your own time, come back into your conscious mind and become aware of your feet on the floor, and your hands in your lap.

Nice and slowly, wriggle your fingers and your toes.

Begin to allow yourself to return back to the outside space.

Take several deep breaths and have a big stretch.

Raising Your Awareness of Why You Respond to Things the Way You Do

Have you ever been in a team, or reported to a boss, where you kept responding negatively to whatever was being proposed or put forward?

I was once in a team where I never felt completely part of the team, or even that my boss particularly liked me. It wasn't until much later, when I had a better awareness of myself, that I realised that 'being liked' was something that I needed to believe and feel to work effectively.

When I did the values exercise in the last chapter, it became very clear to me that 'being liked' is high on my values list.

Even though the work was great and overall I loved what I did, I often felt that I was the odd one out and not fully appreciated.

Looking back, I can see a lot of this was due to a couple of things that happened very soon after I joined the team. As 'being liked' was something I needed at the time, I would generally do whatever was asked. A few times my boss asked me to take on some extra work to help out the team.

At one point, I had a choice of two tasks, and duly chose one. After researching what was required, but before I had invested too much effort or time, my boss asked me to take on a different task because he had the impression that I didn't mind what I did. The task I had already investigated was to be given to another team member, who had decided they didn't want to work on the other task.

Now, truthfully, I didn't mind, but suddenly my 'fairness' filter kicked in. I felt that it wasn't 'fair' that I was being asked to swap just because another member of the team didn't want to do the other task! From that moment on my radar was up to what was fair or not. And unfortunately, my radar also went crazy when the team member in question wasn't available or didn't put their hand up to do something.

My sense of 'fairness' was not being met, I felt threatened, and that influenced my behaviour in that team. It wasn't pretty, but at the time I wasn't aware of it. If I had been, my responses could have been much more resourceful.

David Rock, who created the SCARF model of social threats and rewards, talks about two themes emerging from social neuroscience:

1. Much of the motivation driving social behaviour is governed by an overarching organising principle of minimising threat and maximising reward.
2. The brain deals with social needs in much the same way as the need for food and water.

The SCARF model[4]

The SCARF model summarises these two themes within a framework that captures the common factors that can activate a reward or threat response in social situations. These five domains of human social experience are: Status, Certainty, Autonomy, Relatedness, and Fairness.

---

[4] Definitions taken from Rock, D. (2008). 'SCARF: A brain-based model for collaborating with and influencing others', *NeuroLeadership Journal, 1*, 44–52.

Figure 9: The SCARF Model

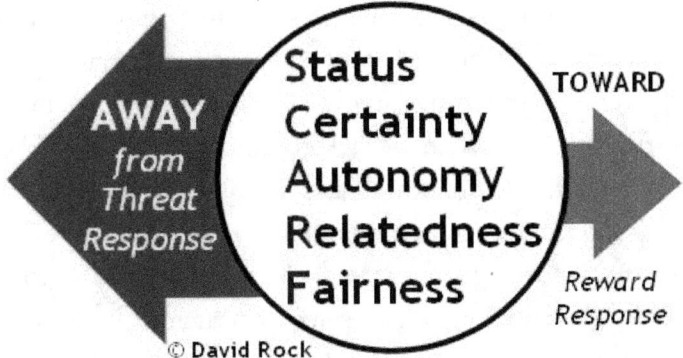

- Status is about relative importance, 'pecking order', and seniority. Two key aspects of our brain's perception of status are:
  1) How easily a threat response can be triggered by such conventional workplace practices as performance reviews and 'feedback' conversations
  2) The fact that threat and reward responses related to changes in status can be triggered 'even when the stakes are meaningless'.

  These dynamics imply not only that extreme care must be taken to conduct reviews and provide feedback in ways designed to boost, rather than threaten, the recipient's status, but also that attention must be paid to all the little, everyday ways in which interpersonal status can be built up and torn down.

- Certainty concerns being able to predict the future. The importance of certainty can be seen as a result of the brain's effort to conserve energy, which derives from the limited capacity of the prefrontal cortex, the seat of executive function.

We resist dedicating mental effort to decision-making and impulse control because we're preserving resources in case we need them more urgently in the next moment, and the same dynamic contributes to our resistance to uncertainty. When we act with sufficient certainty, our brain senses patterns, successfully predicts next steps, and operates much more efficiently. But when we lack certainty and can't predict what will happen next, 'the brain must use dramatically more resources, involving the more energy-intensive prefrontal cortex, to process moment-to-moment experience.' That said, it's useful to distinguish mild uncertainty from excessive uncertainty. The former triggers a mild threat response, generating just enough adrenaline and dopamine to spark curiosity and energise people to solve problems. However, when perceived uncertainty gets out of hand, people panic and make bad decisions.

- Autonomy provides a sense of control over events. Our perception of our ability to exert control over our environment has a substantial effect on our response to stress factors in our life. When we feel more autonomous, we're much more resistant to stress and when we feel less autonomous, we can perceive the same set of circumstances as much more stressful.

  Two aspects of autonomy worth noting are: 1) autonomy and certainty are intertwined; more autonomy yields a greater sense of certainty about the future; and 2) similar to status, even a subtle perception of autonomy can help, suggesting that even where autonomy is substantially limited by organisational constraints, meaningful perceptions of autonomy can be generated by small gestures.

- Relatedness is a sense of safety with others, of friend rather than foe.

Our ability to feel trust and empathy for others is shaped by whether our brain perceives them to be part of the same social group as us. When a new person is perceived as different, the information travels along neural pathways that are associated with discomfort (as opposed to the neural pathways triggered by people who are perceived as similar to oneself, which are associated with comfort).

When people begin to make a stronger social connection, their brains secrete a hormone called oxytocin in each other's presence. This chemical, which has been linked with affection, maternal behaviour, sexual arousal, and generosity, disarms the threat response and further activates the neural networks that permit us to perceive someone as 'just like us'.

What this means is that in an interpersonal setting it's important to interact in ways that will surface points of similarity, strengthen social connections, and increase a sense of relatedness. From a neuroscientific perspective, this process generates oxytocin, allows our brains to classify the other person as 'friend' rather than 'foe', and contributes to feelings of trust and empathy.

- Fairness is a perception of fair exchanges between people. The perception that an event has been unfair generates a strong response in the brain, stirring hostility and undermining trust. In organisations, the perception of unfairness creates an environment in which trust and collaboration cannot flourish. Unfair exchanges generate a strong threat response that can elicit such intense emotions as disgust. When a person perceives another person as unfair, they will not feel empathy for their pain, and may even feel rewarded when they are punished.

  As with status, perceptions of fairness are relative. This means that in any given disagreement there is no absolute truth to be discovered, and the logical arguments of either side are bound to be fruitless.

Andrew O'Keeffe, author of *Hardwired Humans*, describes how the avoidance of loss is a far greater motivator to humans than the opportunity to gain. He says we are wired to first screen for pain and danger rather than seek pleasure. If we were wired for pleasure above pain we would not survive at all, as screening for pain and danger keeps us out of harm's way.

He explains how we screen information for loss versus gain; we support change if we detect a gain, we resist change if we detect loss. And in the case of uncertainty, the default is to assume a loss. We make this assessment at an individual level, and it means that when we are being reviewed or receiving feedback we focus and dwell on the negative as a defence against loss.

When you have been confronted with a change – maybe a new team structure, a new way of doing something or a new role – how have you responded? As mentioned in my previous example, I responded badly when confronted with a loss – the loss of being liked or respected – even though it was only a perception.

We tend to assume loss at times of change, and we are most concerned about:

- Will my job be secure?
- Who will I be reporting to?
- Will the membership of my team change?

Loss aversion explains why employees get annoyed over things like losing their permanent desks and having to move to flexi-desking. They are losing the certainty of whom they sit with and where.

We often hear that people don't like change. However, it's not change itself that is the problem, it's the risk of personal loss from that change. When we first hear about a change we instantly decide at an individual level, filtered by our immediate emotional response, whether this change should be classified as gain or loss. If we detect gain we support the change. If we detect loss or are unsure, we resist. And once we have made that classification, we are unlikely to alter it.

In workplaces the forms of loss or potential loss are many and varied. There are the obvious ones such as loss of income, loss of benefits, and loss of role through redundancy or loss of role through demotion or restructuring. There is the potential for loss of social standing through social embarrassment or even humiliation. For loss of routine or of the familiar. For loss of subject-matter expertise if systems and processes change. Loss can even be experienced just by someone else gaining something.

The impact of this neural dynamic is often visible in organisations. For example, when leaders trigger a threat response, employees' brains become much less efficient. When leaders make people feel good about themselves, clearly communicate their expectations, give employees latitude to make decisions, support people's efforts to build good relationships, and treat the whole organisation fairly, it prompts a reward response.

Others in the organisation become more effective, more open to ideas, and more creative. They notice the kind of information that might have passed them by if fear or resentment had been making it difficult to focus their attention. They are less susceptible to burnout because they are able to manage their stress. They feel intrinsically rewarded.

Knowing the drivers that can cause a threat response enables people to design interactions to minimise threats. For example, knowing that a lack of autonomy activates a genuine threat response, a leader may consciously avoid micromanaging their employees. Secondly, knowing about the drivers that can activate a reward response enables people to motivate others more effectively by tapping into internal rewards, thereby reducing the reliance on external rewards such as money.

We have very little time – approximately one third of a second – after the perception of a potential threat before a neurological threat response is triggered. On an individual basis, it's essential to cultivate our ability to recognise the conditions that might trigger a threat response and proactively reappraise the situation. At the group or interpersonal level, it's important to be aware of the speed and ease with which a threat response can be triggered in someone else, to understand how such a response is likely to undermine effective communication, and to take steps that support the other person's reappraisal of the situation without making them defensive.

Some suggestions are:

- Become familiar with the impact of the five domains of human social experience: Status, Certainty, Autonomy, Relatedness, and Fairness. Think about when these have impacted you, and when you have noticed their impact on others.
- Talk about this concept with your people leader, and let them know that you will highlight to them those times when you feel that something they have done has created a threat response in you.

- When you are confronted with something that you don't like, pause and consider why.
- When you do become aware of making a decision based on loss, review it and consider how it can become a gain.

My questions are:

- Have you ever experienced a threat response in relation to any of the five domains of human social experience?
- How can you reappraise a situation when a threat response has been triggered in you?
- How can you help someone else reappraise a situation without them becoming defensive?
- Think about a time when you experienced a change where you gained. How did you respond to that change?
- Think about a time you experienced a change where you perceived a loss for yourself. How did you respond to that change?
- Think about a job you loved. Why was it so great? Now think about a job you didn't love. Why not?

The First Impressions We Make and Building Rapport

A primary school vice principal hired me to help her change the first impression she was making during interviews. At the time we met, Linda had applied for nine principal roles for various schools in the Melbourne area. In each case she had come second. Applying and interviewing for a school principal role is lengthy, complex, and difficult, so I really felt for her.

It is said that the decision to hire someone, or at least move them to the next round of interviews, is made within 30 seconds of meeting them. We are hardwired to classify people as good or bad, 'like me' or 'not like me'. The vice principal wanted to focus on what impression she was making within that first 30 seconds.

There may have been occasions when you were not as persuasive or as effective as you would have liked. Maybe your idea was not accepted by the person you were seeking to convince. A likely cause of your setback is that you failed to effectively utilise your first few seconds – the moment when the listener 'classified' your idea.

First impressions:

- Are made of people, events, and places within a few seconds.
- Generally occur within the first seven words (the 'working memory' of the brain). To be persuasive, you need to effectively utilise this window. Whatever you say and do in your first seven words will be the main determinant of the response.
- Are mainly driven by the emotion generated in those first few seconds, from which we classify our meaning.

- Are binary in nature (good versus bad, 'like me' versus 'not like me').
- Are unlikely to change once we have made our instant assessment.

The first thing I introduced Linda to was the concept of building rapport with someone, and how to do this within the first few seconds of her interview.

Building rapport

Building rapport as quickly as possible makes the listener feel that you are 'just like them', swaying that instant decision to 'good' rather than 'bad'. An NLP definition for rapport is 'the ability to reduce difference between yourself and another at unconscious levels to promote a harmonious relationship'.

You don't always have to try to build rapport; it happens unconsciously with people we like. Sometimes though, we need to put in some extra effort to connect with people with whom we do not have a previous connection or relationship. We must actively, consciously find ways of building rapport.

Rapport has nothing to do with liking someone; it has nothing to do with agreeing with someone; it is not empathy or mimicking the other person. It is all about building a resourceful relationship between yourself and another. It enables you to build a harmonious relationship with another person to facilitate effective communication.

Building rapport with someone else is about matching their physical gestures and posture. Matching the tone, pace, and volume of their voice. Matching their language. Matching the rhythm and pace of their breath. Matching their values or emotions.

This is something that occurs naturally. If you watch people on public transport who know each other, or people together in a restaurant, the rapport between them is unmistakable – when one leans forward, the other leans forward. When one crosses their legs, the other crosses their legs. There's a rhythm to the way they talk and do things.

By watching a person for non-verbal clues and listening for language patterns, you can adapt your own language and behaviour to harmonise with them and establish a deep level of rapport. This is accomplished through something called 'pacing and leading'.

Everyone has their own model of the world, based on their life experiences. Pacing is the process of using and feeding back key verbal and non-verbal cues from another person in order to match *their* model of the world. Pacing or mirroring a person's non-verbal communication builds a level of rapport that creates sameness and the sense that you are 'just like them'. It allows you to step into their shoes and communicate with them in their own language and through their own way of being.

Leading involves attempting to change, add to, or enrich another person's behaviour or thinking process by subtly shifting your own verbal and behavioural patterns in the desired direction, and having them follow.

You can use the 'pace to lead' concept to test if you are in rapport. After pacing someone and matching them, shift your posture. For example, if you were leaning forward in your chair, lean back. If they match your movement within a minute, try it again, and then again. If they continue to match your movement, you know you have established a level of rapport.

When people consciously build rapport with others, and practise rapport building until they become unconsciously skilled at it, then all forms of communication become easier and more effective regardless of whom they are communicating with.

Think back to your work environment. Do you avoid communicating with certain people at work because you don't like them or you just feel they are not on the same wavelength as you? Try building rapport with them –

you may be surprised with the results.

For a few years while my children were in primary school I worked on a school council, and even became the president for a couple of years (chaired the meetings) after the incumbent president quit suddenly due to a disagreement with the council and school principal.

Some of the parents and teachers on the council were very difficult to deal with. Many had joined the council primarily to meet their own agendas, which were often in direct conflict with the overall council agenda. I used to feel physically ill every time the council met due to anxiety about what these councillors would do or say to disrupt our meetings.

Once I learned about rapport, particularly matching body language and pacing and leading, our council meetings ran more smoothly. I consciously built rapport with one parent in particular, then each other member of the council around the table, so in a short time everyone was in rapport. We could allow differences of opinion to coexist with positive intent so that meetings no longer degenerated into discussions about personality.

Remember Linda, the vice principal who had been coming second in all the interviews she attended? So how did she go at building rapport?

She was really curious about the concept of rapport and was happy to try it out. She chose to practise with her new school principal, with whom she had a difficult relationship. As vice principal she had always been the sounding board for her previous principal, and this wasn't the case with the new principal, who was reluctant to share any information with her.

Within a week of explaining how to build rapport, I heard from Linda, who asked me 'How do I turn this rapport thing off?' After practising building rapport with her principal and really entering her model of the world, Linda found that that the principal was sharing everything with her. In fact, she was sharing *too much* information, personal as well as work-related, and Linda was finding it difficult to get a moment to herself.

The great news is that soon afterwards Linda was successful at obtaining a principal role at another school.

Another client, Sam, was also willing to learn how to consciously apply rapport. Sam was a country-based corporate manager who wanted to make some large changes to her life because what she was doing wasn't working anymore. She wanted to learn how to build rapport with everyone she came into contact with.

Up to a point Sam had been doing a reasonable job at managing her satellite business despite some challenging circumstances. Actually, her team was so dysfunctional that I'm surprised they managed to do all the great business they did! As soon as Sam learnt how to consciously build rapport, she found that all her relationships with family and the people she worked with changed, often in subtle ways. For want of a better word, they became 'easier'. She felt they understood her better, and she understood them better.

How you can build rapport

Body Rapport

- Match posture.
- Match breathing.
- Match gestures.
- Match eye blink rate.
- Match spinal tilt.

Voice Rapport

- Match tone/pitch.
- Match volume.
- Match speed.

Language

- Match visual language.
- Match auditory language.
- Match kinaesthetic language.

Some suggestions are:

- This is something you can play with and become passionate about. Go out of your way to build rapport with each and every person you meet, everyone you talk to on the phone, even those people that you communicate with via email or other written correspondence.
- Reduce differences at unconscious levels to create a harmonious relationship. Become known as that person who somehow gets

along with everyone!
- Wherever you are, notice the people around you. Notice if groups of people are in rapport.

My questions are:

- Is there someone with whom you have a difficult relationship that you would like to improve?
- How do you know what sort of first impressions you are making?

Can We Consciously Create Trust with Someone?

The Cambridge Dictionary definition of trust is 'to believe that someone is good and honest and will not harm you, or that something is safe and reliable'.

Trust occurs naturally. We may find ourselves trusting someone we have just met. Yet we'll meet someone else and find ourselves mistrusting them. This is because a level of matching occurs unconsciously that determines how much we trust someone. As discussed in the previous chapter, this relates to the level of rapport.

Do we need to trust someone to be able to work with them?

The short answer is yes. Trust is required in any interaction we have with others if we are to reach an effective outcome. This is particularly true when we are part of a team.

A term used a lot in corporations is 'high-performance teams'. This means teams that are highly focused on their goals, achieve superior results, and outperform similar teams.

There is no question that the high-performance teams I have worked with and observed have a high degree of trust between all team members. They watch each other's backs; have a diversity of skills and competencies to complement each other; have a diverse range of opinions, which they openly share; and communicate consistently about any issues that affect the team.

Without trust, the team is just a group of individuals doing their own thing. It doesn't matter how capable or talented each of those individuals is, if trust isn't present between them the team will not reach its full potential.

Normally people believe that trust is either there or not there, without considering if it is a skill that can be learnt. Trust can be actively managed but it generally only comes up in discussions when it has been breached.

Building trust is like building a bridge: without the foundation and engineering, it may fail. As someone wanting to move into a more senior role, it is essential that you understand the building blocks for trust and how to initiate these within the team or teams you are part of.

The three trust building blocks: capability, communication, and collaboration.

Figure 10: Trust Building Blocks

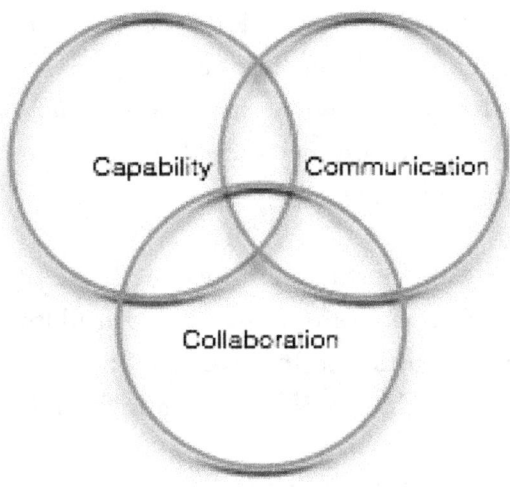

Capability

Team members must trust that their teammates are competent and can successfully complete the tasks relevant to the team's success.

Recall the model at the beginning of this book where I explained ability and confidence. If someone is in the high confidence and low ability quadrant, or the low confidence and low ability quadrant, then my level of trust in their competence will be low.

In a high-performance team, each team member should be able to focus on their own tasks without worrying about teammates following through with their assigned tasks. Team members must realise when they need help and ask for it, instead of concealing weaknesses from the group. When team members show vulnerability to their teammates and the teammates respond in an efficient and helpful manner, trust will grow between them.

Communication

Consistent and meaningful communication is necessary for a trusting relationship within a team. If one team member discovers vital information that is relevant to the team's success, such as a deadline change or a lack of resources, they should communicate it to the other members as soon as possible.

People who work within virtual teams need to make an effort to keep all members within the loop. For example, an email addressed to one or two team members is not sufficient. Instead, a group email or the use of an online collaboration tool is necessary to communicate with every member.

Team members who receive communication from other team members should always respond to confirm that they have received the information and build trust.

Collaboration

True collaboration won't happen without a sense of trust between team members. When team members collaborate, they share creative ideas without fear that another team member will take credit for their ideas. Team members who feel they are in a trusting team environment may also be more willing to bring up concerns that are relevant to the team's goals or members.

A collaborative and trusting team environment allows team members to share personal information and develop a stronger bond with their teammates.

Without all three building blocks, team members can fail to meet expectations and cause mistrust. This can be because team members are not capable of doing their job (failed capability); because the expectations were not communicated or understood properly (failed communication); or because team members have acted with bad intent or dishonesty (failed collaboration).

Your personal leadership effectiveness grows out of trustworthiness. To lead others effectively, you must first be able to lead yourself effectively. As you demonstrate trustworthiness, other people will begin to trust you as a leader.

Some people are very successful at building trust into their interpersonal relationships. How do they do it? Does it just come naturally for some people and not others?

Effective professional businesspeople, like professional athletes, do not rely solely on skills that 'come naturally'.

Instead, they do two things:

1. They analyse their behaviour to find out what is working for them and what isn't.
2. They practise until they are so accustomed to the new skill that, when it really matters, they instinctively recreate that skill.

They learn what works, then practise it until it feels familiar.

I have described the three building blocks of team trust: capability, communication, and collaboration. But *how* can you create these? The four elements that combine to create trust are around what you do, not what you feel or what your intentions are: *reliability*, *acceptance*, *openness*, and *congruence*.

Your feelings and intentions are important but they are not visible. People can only trust you for what you do – your actions.

Creating trust

Figure 11: Elements of Trust

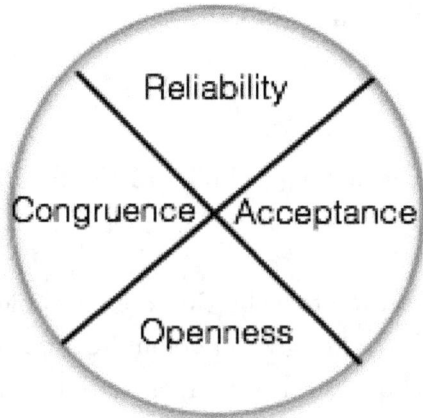

Reliability

People we relate to want to know if we do what we say we will do. It is pretty hard to have confidence in a person who makes promises they don't keep.

Don't make promises you can't keep, even if you think it will smooth over the situation temporarily, or appease an angry situation. In the long run it will hurt you. Do what you say you will do, and if you can't or won't do it, don't say you will.

Reliability means following up and seeing through the promises and commitments you make. It means 'I'll do what I say I'll do.'

If you work with someone that has a problem with reliability, say something! A colleague I worked with was always late for our meetings, which made me feel that she didn't value my time. I started to become resentful and was reluctant to set up meetings with her. I finally explained how I felt: that she wasn't reliable. She was horrified, and rectified the situation from that moment on.

Acceptance

As necessary as reliability is, it will not build trust in the interpersonal relationship by itself.

Everyone wants to be accepted for who they are, not judged, criticised, or made to feel inferior. It is easy to give a person the impression that they are slightly stupid or inadequate for not understanding some aspect of the family, company, department, or project as well as you.

Or, a person may feel 'put down' by the use of technical jargon, obscure references, or accusations of guilt that they are not aware of or familiar with.

Accept each person for who they are, without judgment or criticism.

Each person, as long as he or she is relating to you, is okay, and it is up to you to let them know that when you are with them, they are the most important person in the world.

Openness

People tend to want to cooperate best with people who will level with them, not hide anything and give them the whole story (even if some of the details may be unpleasant).

People can take good news or bad news, but they can't take surprises. If you discover there has been a change of plans that affects another person, or you are unhappy with someone's work results, then they should be the first to know.

They will respect and trust you more for your openness.

Congruence

Congruence is the knowledge that what you say is on track with what you believe, what you know to be true, and what you do.

You will remember in an earlier chapter we already talked about being congruent, or walking your talk, in terms of our three brains (head, heart, and gut).

Congruence means saying and doing what you believe, being straightforward and honest, and saying what is true even if it is unpleasant and not exactly what you think the other person wants to hear.

Sometimes a person will be so gentle that their real message is not fully communicated. They are not doing this out of malice, but out of consideration for the other person. However, it is not congruent and people intuitively sense this.

Take the four elements – reliability, acceptance, openness, and congruence – and apply them to your relationships. You will find that you are the kind of person people want to relate to.

An important fact to always bear in mind is that three of the four elements are not enough. In order to build lasting, ongoing relationships, all four are necessary. Trust often takes a long time to build but, unfortunately, only an instant to destroy.

Some suggestions are:

- Consider teams you have been part of, and how the building blocks of trust have applied to each team.
- Consider the personal elements of trust and how they apply to your individual relationships.

My questions are:

- Have you ever been part of a high-performance team? If so, were all the building blocks in place (capability, communication, collaboration)?
- Have you ever failed to deliver on someone else's expectations? If so, which of the three building blocks failed?
- Consider the four elements of personal trust (reliability, acceptance, openness, congruence). Give yourself a rating out of 10 for each element (with 10 being expert) at home, and at work.
- Consider a time when someone lost your trust. Which of the four elements can explain this?

In Corporations, Who You Know Is as Important as What You Know!

Our ability to step into more senior roles is increased when our level of confidence meets our ability to influence. Our awareness of others and ourselves is wrapped around our ability to network and build relationships.

Your ability to influence others, help others, and get help yourself is reflected by who you know inside and outside of your organisation.

- It may help you get promoted.
- It may help you in your role.
- It may help you understand the organisation and how it works more strategically.

I'm not talking about networking.

There are a few events I love going to, to reconnect with people I have known for years but never seem to find time to see. But other than having a lovely time and meeting lovely people (although that's not guaranteed), I'm yet to get any real value from of turning up to an 'event'. Maybe it's just me, I just don't get it. I don't want to end the night with a heap of business cards for people I barely know, which I have no intention of using. Even when I do make a connection with someone I like and catch up, it's usually all pretty pointless.

I do love a good speaker and there are some great events around at the moment that choose their speakers very well. But at the end of the event, having had breakfast (or in the evening, a glass of wine), I am the one making a beeline for the door as soon as the speaker finishes, before the networking starts!

For women in leadership, this isn't what I mean when I talk about 'who you know'. I am talking about the one-on-one connections you make with people to build strong relationships. These connections can assist you, support you, and guide you. They can introduce you to other people they think will be a great connection for you. These connections could lead into mentoring or sponsoring relationships.

Connecting well is like stepping on an escalator and fast tracking up through levels.

Connecting within your organisation is about finding out who works where, who knows who, and how the organisation fits together.

Having worked in large corporations for many years, sometimes I find that I just don't 'get' what other areas do – which means I don't know how to tap into their expertise if I need it. I love to learn about other areas and find out how everything fits together. Then when I do connect with new people, I become a connector myself and direct them to connect with other people if they have a particular problem they would like to solve.

The other thing I am very aware of is that the people we know in an organisation, or anywhere, we don't *really* know.

You get that don't you?

How often have you caught up with someone and, when they shared something about themselves, been surprised to find that you didn't actually know they were a bricklayer, a lawyer, a marathon runner, great with Excel… or whatever the case may have been.

People often end up in roles through pure luck. I don't know many people who are in their current role due to a plan and goals that they put in place years before.

I once had to assist with a career expo, and in preparation I mapped out my career and the roles I have had. Even I was surprised with the number of career changes I have had over my working life. My first job was as a truck driver transporting harvested wheat from the family farm to the local silos, and my second as a Girl Friday (yes, that title really did exist) with a Forestry Commission in a small rural town. My main job there was tracking logging requirements in forests and leasing bee sites!

Then I moved to the big smoke and started nursing at a large trauma hospital. Next I moved onto banking and finance, followed by my own coaching and training business. Very few people would know the breadth and depth of my career.

What about yours?

We are natural connectors; however, hierarchies, politics, and silos often stymie this. The more we can connect with others, the greater the likelihood of building relationships and bridging some of those hierarchies and silos. This means connecting with people at different levels of seniority to you.

Just because someone is more junior than you doesn't mean they don't have something to offer, and just because someone is more senior than you doesn't mean you don't have something to offer.

Some interactions within a corporation can be invisible to others. You never know where a connection will take you, so maintain your network and continue to grow it.

A client of mine was reluctant to connect with people in more senior roles, as she didn't want to 'waste their time'. This was someone who was being groomed for a senior role and needed to find senior mentors. When she eventually started making connections with senior leaders in different areas of her organisation, she was pleasantly surprised by how helpful they all were. More importantly, she realised the value *she* brought to the table by assisting them in different areas.

The larger the organisation, the more important it is to have a breadth of connections throughout it.

Here are some suggestions:

- Look around your organisation and identify areas that you don't know much about. Find someone you can connect with in that area and set up a meeting to find out more about what the area does.
- If you have a mentor within your organisation, ask them for the names of people you can connect to, and ask them to introduce you.

My questions are:

- How many people in your company do you know well enough to be able to call up and talk to?
- Are there areas within your organisation that you are totally clueless about?
- How savvy are you on how your organisation fits together – who's at the top, and what does the structure look like?

Successful mentoring

Mentoring is defined as an enduring partnership in creative collaboration, professional growth, and personal development. It helps the mentee develop new skills, gives the mentor the opportunity to leave a legacy, and allows both to experience intergenerational and cross-cultural interaction.

Mentors are more significant than other teachers – mentors influence us in profound ways.

Evidence shows that people who are mentored do better in their career. For women, this is important, as a mentor can provide encouragement and support at the beginning of a change in career or leadership level, or help with the return to work following extended leave, such as maternity leave.

As stated by Dr Pamela Matters (1994),

> A successful mentoring partnership is defined as a close relationship between two people where the mentor guides and assists the mentoree to a level of personal and professional excellence not attained previously. The tangible aspects are easily observable – new skills learned, ideas exchanged, enhancement of personal performance, and increased knowledge of a specific area of human endeavour.
>
> The intangible aspects are more difficult to perceive but they are noticeably felt because there is always a close emotional bonding between participants, which provides strength to the partnership structure in this essential relationship. The success of the mentoring relationship rests on the mutual excitement the mentor and mentoree have about a particular field and the commonality

of their own working and learning styles. In the most successful partnerships, participants achieve intellectual and creative growth with shared ideas acting as a stimulus for that growth.

One of the biggest benefits of mentoring is that it helps people learn from their mistakes. A mentor can be honest about where the person being mentored might have gone wrong and help address that. Mentors can also help to identify skills that might be useful in a new role, and help the mentee to learn and hone them.

Some organisations have formal mentoring programs, where junior team members are appointed to more experienced, usually more senior mentors. If you have access to such a program, tap into this resource and make the best use of it.

However, even when formal programs exist, I find that an informal mentor can be even better. That is, the mentor you find yourself, whom you have contacted and checked for their availability.

If you are not used to contacting senior leaders, it may be a bit scary to make that first contact, and ask for some mentoring support. Even people who are very confident and capable in their role can struggle with this.

When you establish a mentoring relationship, it is crucial to have a mutual understanding of what each person wants to achieve, and to establish boundaries early on. Your mentor's role is to give advice and listen to your concerns, not to find or secure your next role.

Confidentiality is imperative as the basis for a successful mentoring relationship. Without trust, the mentee may feel vulnerable, particularly if the mentor is well connected or good friends with the mentee's boss.

In the previous section I mentioned a client who was reluctant to connect with people in more senior roles for fear of wasting their time. But to understand how other areas of the organisation worked, and to seek advice on how to take the next step up, finding mentors outside of her specific area of expertise was essential. She actually ended up with several mentors, though she admits some were more useful than others. Some of those initial mentoring relationships are ongoing, while others served a particular purpose at the time, then naturally ended.

For many organisations, establishing mentor relationships between senior and junior staff members is one of the best ways to build a culture of collaboration and to tap into the knowledge capital held within the organisation.

Mentoring is, or can be, a two-way learning experience. As a mentee, you learn from the skills and experience of the mentor. But the mentor is learning some important skills as well – how to advise, coach, lead, and manage.

The fast pace of change within organisations can sometimes cause people to feel unsettled and damage morale. Mentoring can provide guidance, advice, sponsoring, and a role model who validates your actions, motivates you, protects you, and transfers culture.

For the mentor, the partnership provides the opportunity to confirm, renew, and share their experience and knowledge.

Some guidelines in seeking out a mentor:

- Think about why you want to work with a mentor. What goals are you trying to achieve from a mentoring relationship? Are there gaps

in your skill base that a mentor could help with?
- Consider the attributes you would like in a mentor. For example, do you have a particular business focus, or an area of the organisation you want to find out more about? A mentor is someone who has already done what you are seeking to develop or achieve, so who do you know that has the necessary skills or experience? Who do you know that knows that person and can introduce you?
- Ensure confidentiality, for both you and the mentor
- Consider suitable arrangements or logistics regarding meeting (for instance, how often do you want to meet and will it be by phone or face to face)?
- Be aware at all times that this is a voluntary and optional relationship, so value the mentor's time and come to all meetings prepared with what you want to discuss.

Some guidelines to consider if you are approached to be a mentor:

- How enthusiastic are you about your work? Your enthusiasm will ignite a similar enthusiasm in others. If you are not enthusiastic about your work, you may not be a suitable mentor as this time.
- Are you able and willing to explore and share the expectations, concepts, 'tools', and practices of your role?
- Are you committed to continuous learning, and are you comfortable with challenge?
- Do you have the ability to build trust and rapport in diverse situations?
- Ensure confidentiality, for both you and the person to be mentored.

In addition, as a mentor, you need to be genuinely committed to the partnership, and undertake your role in a way that gives the person you are mentoring the confidence and opportunity to map their own pathway; to motivate themselves and take risks; and to develop through a rich diversity of experiences, including mistakes.

Being suitable for a mentoring role is more about your qualities, skills, and attributes than your years of experience, specific knowledge, or position.

Mentoring someone doesn't need to be an elaborate exercise; it should become a way of life, which is why a natural connection is so important. The relationship needs to be comfortable, not demanding.

Here are some suggestions:

- If you are a bit stuck in your career, find one or two mentors outside of your immediate team as a great way to kick off some different ideas.
- Find a way to be introduced to the person you are seeking as a mentor; it's always easier to make a warm call rather than a cold call! Then be as clear as you can with them about why they would be a great mentor for you.
- If someone has asked you to mentor them, ask them what it is they are specifically looking to achieve.

My questions are:

- Have you ever been mentored (formally or informally)? And if not, why not?
- What would you need to get the most out of a mentoring relationship (either as a mentor, or as a mentee)?

Finding a sponsor

Mentoring and sponsoring can sometimes be confused as the same thing.

As mentioned in the previous section, mentors are familiar with the road that the person being mentored wants to follow. They have been there and done it. They can guide, support, and advise.

Sponsors, who can also be mentors, are advocates in positions of authority who use their influence intentionally to help others advance. Corporations work very much with who knows whom, and who recommends whom. People would much rather hire or fill roles with people who have been endorsed by someone they know (or know of) and respect.

Sponsors are becoming increasingly important. With the move to more diversity in organisations, particularly gender diversity, women have an opportunity to seek out roles that they may not have previously considered. They can advance their careers by developing relationships with sponsors who can then provide confident endorsements.

Sponsorship is talked about much less than mentoring, but it is equally important. A sponsor is someone who will put you forward for new positions and be your advocate when you are pursuing new opportunities. Building a relationship with a sponsor is about building your credibility with them. Someone will not put your name forward or speak up for you unless they trust that you can do what is being asked. Their reputation is on the line.

A sponsor isn't someone you will necessarily catch up with regularly, as you do with your mentors. However, it is important that they believe in your abilities, understand your career aspirations, and know enough about you to be able to speak on your behalf.

From my experience, a sponsor may be someone you work for currently or have done in the past. My most recent sponsor was my manager. He had recently joined our team and it became apparent pretty quickly that the skill sets he was looking for from me weren't ones that I could provide (analytical, number crunching – yuck!). To his credit, he quickly worked out my aspirations and my skills, and actively endorsed me for a role that I attained and thoroughly enjoyed.

You may need to ask someone to be your sponsor, but it should be someone you know well who would be willing to write you a recommendation, which requires them to have a clear understanding of who you are, your professional qualities, and what you aspire to be.

My suggestions are:

- Find people who have influence and know your strengths, abilities, and aspirations.
- Build strong relationships with both your manager and their manager.
- Keep your development plan up to date and keep honing it to be a true reflection of who you are and what you want to achieve.

My questions are:

- Who do you know right now who will actively sponsor you?
- Do you currently have a mentor who would be happy to endorse you for other roles or speak on your behalf in the areas you are

interested in moving to?
- What is preventing you from finding some sponsors?

Hierarchies, Silos, and Politics

I love these three words. They exemplify corporate life. If you have spent any time as an employee in a corporation, you probably know what I mean.

Large organisations require hierarchies, which can be conceptualised as similar to 'tribes'. It is suggested that a tribe should be no larger than 150 people to be effective.

As Andrew O'Keeffe wrote in *Hardwired Humans*, 'Humans are social animals. We are hardwired to connect strongest to our family-sized group of around seven people in our "village" of up to 150 people. In large organisations people will have much stronger bonds with their small team and their unit than they will with the wider organisation.'

Without hierarchies large organisations would find it very difficult to function.

One of the drawbacks of having a hierarchy is that once you have layers reporting up into other layers you cannot avoid the development of silos.

I grew up on a farm where we used silos to store grain after it was harvested. My father and brothers used the silos to separate different sorts of grain. These aren't unlike the type of silos I mean when I talk about organisation silos.

These organisational silos are used to separate areas of the organisation. For example, an organisation may have a finance area, a sales area, a marketing area, and a product area. When people don't interact well with people outside of their 'silo' it makes it difficult to get things done, to be agile and nimble. Silos make it very difficult to embrace change.

Once you have hierarchies and silos, politics aren't far behind. Organisational politics involve the pursuit of individual agendas and self-interest within an organisation without considering or caring about its effect on the organisation's values or goals.

All organisations, to a greater or lesser extent, have to deal with politics. Managing this landscape requires awareness of its existence, who the players are, and the rules of the game.

Figure 12: Hierarchies, Politics, and Silos

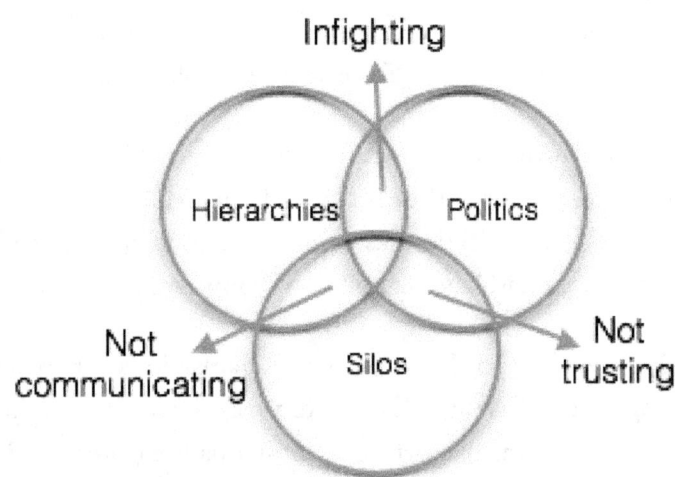

Hierarchies

The definition of a hierarchy is 'any system of persons or things ranked one above another.'

Every organization has levels – a team and their manager are two levels. The manager reports to someone else, creating a third level; that person reports to someone else to create a fourth level, and so on. The larger the organisation, the more levels, ranging from the Chief Executive Officer (CEO) through to new graduates starting at the very bottom of the organisation.

If you have been part of a corporation you will know how frustrating it can be to deal with several chains of command, as it can make it very difficult to get things done quickly. Start-ups are generally much more nimble as they have a flatter structure.

There is generally good communication between two adjacent levels in a hierarchy and, depending on the organisation, sometimes between three. From my experience, there is very little connection or communication beyond this. Logistically, of course, this is unavoidable as there are only so many people you can interact with for effective results at any time.

In theory, messages from above cascade down through the levels. A senior leader briefs his direct reports; they then brief their direct reports, and so on. This works well if each leader has a good relationship and structure to pass these messages on and has the ability to communicate effectively.

There is absolutely a need for hierarchies in organisations. There are real benefits to being able to manage a large number of people by breaking them down into small teams reporting to individual managers, and there is no effective alternative just yet.

Hierarchies allow you to identify who you want to get access to. A top-down hierarchy creates a picture of an organisation – who fits where, and who does what.

This can also have drawbacks. In the past I've found that if a person I needed to connect with perceived me as more junior, they were less likely to accept a meeting request.

Has that ever happened to you?

What happened to everyone being part of one organisation? There is also the perception – or perhaps reality – that you can't bypass your boss to speak to their boss!

It is great to see the introduction of 'skip' level meetings, where a level is 'skipped' and team members meet their boss's boss one on one. This is only effective if trust has been established between all levels.

As someone wanting to step up into more senior roles, understanding the hierarchy of the organisation is essential to target the areas you are interested in and identify whom you should be contacting and building relationships with. When you belong to an organisation, the ability to build connections with levels above, below, and outside your current position is critical to your personal success as well as the success of the company.

Understanding the hierarchy also strengthens your awareness about where people fit and what they do. Though it may be difficult to get to speak with someone several levels from where you currently reside, it is possible – though initially it will be easier to choose someone a maximum of two levels above you.

Some suggestions are:

- Review the structure of your organisation and develop an understanding of how each area fits in.
- Within your area, have a look at the hierarchy and consider if you are familiar with what people do outside of your immediate team.
- Find an area that you would like to know more about and identify one or two people who are currently a bit more senior than you. Contact those people and find out more about what they do.

My questions are:

- Consider where you are now and review who you know two levels above and two levels below you. Are these people you are comfortable to have a conversation with?
- If the hierarchy has been restructured within your organisation or team, why do you think this occurred?

Silos

Silos are insidious and difficult to break down, and link to politics at all levels.

As an individual there are lots of ways to punch holes in these silos. It comes down to connecting. Create connections between levels by developing mentoring relationships, networking, and finding out what is happening in other areas. The biggest benefit is that you will often find short cuts for doing things from unexpected areas.

Silos exist whenever the functional role of a team or a business unit is defined. Similar to hierarchies, which limit connections between vertical levels, silos limit connections between horizontal divisions. I may be an expert in one section, but have no awareness of the expertise required in a different section. So I may feel that I have no need or time to find out what it does.

The difference between hierarchies and silos is that the former is built into the organisational structure, while the latter occurs based on the level of connectedness between areas.

I experienced silos for the first time in my first banking role. I became part of a new business unit set up to make innovations within the electronic banking (the term at the time) area. This was a new and emerging area. The products we were promoting, or looking at how to enhance, actually belonged to another part of that organisation. The silos mentality was so strong that we were instructed not to talk to the people in those teams. And they had been told not to support or help us. It was beyond ridiculous and, at my very junior level, difficult to believe. Eventually the whole area was disbanded and absorbed into the mainstream part of the bank.

A high-performance team is great for an organisation – *if* they are able to look outside of their area and be inclusive of other areas.

Silos can also be geographical. I live and work in Melbourne, and in some of my previous jobs there has been a clear 'them and us' mentality when it comes to people in other cities (for instance, Sydney). This even occurs when different teams are located in different buildings within the one city!

The silos in the role I mentioned above, when we couldn't even talk to the people who owned the products we were trying to develop, were also partly geographic in nature as we had our own (small) building in a pretty groovy area, and we used Apple computers while the rest of the organisation was on PCs. No wonder no one outside of our team would talk to us!

Silos usually form because employees have more loyalty to their group than the organisation they work for. When this starts to happen the silos solidify: team members become insular and sometimes distrustful of other business areas. And of course, once trust disappears (if it was even there to begin with) it becomes more and more difficult for groups to communicate effectively and work together.

If you are looking to step up, either in your existing area or in another area of your organisation, you need to become aware of these silos and find ways to bridge them.

If only everyone in an organisation built relationships both within and outside of their immediate team, the level of effective communication would improve immensely, as well as the level of trust. That is why it is so hard to get stuff done in an organisation – too few people know enough about what other areas do; they are too busy focusing on their own patch.

Some suggestions are:

- Build your network. The larger your network, the more effective your understanding of the organisation. Knowing people in various areas within the organisation, and making sure they know you, is a simple way to break down silos.
- As well as knowing people in other areas, focus on how you can build higher levels of trust with them so they will be willing to assist you if you require help.

My questions are:

- Which areas of your organisation do you find it more difficult to tap into?
- Are there particular silos that you think are stronger than others? How could you begin to break the walls down?
- Who do you know that could introduce you to people in those areas?
- Do you feel locked into the area you are currently in, due to your expertise, familiarity with your role, or unfamiliarity with areas outside of it?
- Do you limit what you think you can do because of the area you are in?

Politics

We have now considered hierarchies and silos, which are naturally occurring structures within an organisation. Politics are the spinoff from these.

The degree of politics in an organisation is dependent on the level of connectedness of employees to an organisation's vision and values; the level of communication both vertically through the hierarchy and horizontally through the divisions (or silos); and the level of trust between all of these.

As mentioned at the beginning of this section, organisational politics involves the pursuit of individual agendas and self-interest within an organisation without considering or caring about its effect on the organisation's values, vision, or goals. All organisations, to a greater or lesser extent, have to deal with politics.

Dealing with your organisations politics can be exhausting. Consider the following:

- Rely on facts and have the data to back you up when you enter into a political argument. This can defuse any political positioning.
- Build up your network within your organisation. The more people that know you and trust you, the more likely you will know what is going on within the political landscape.
- Be comfortable admitting when you are wrong. The power of being able to admit mistakes is huge in an organisation that is driven by political agendas. This can completely defuse a tense, politically charged situation in an instant. However, also be aware that if you are wrong too often, it destroys your credibility and the perception

of your competence.
- Think about what is being asked, and the reasons behind that. A question in a politically charged environment is rarely the simple question it seems. Try to understand where the question is leading to so you can anticipate and adjust as needed.
- And just as you should admit when you are wrong, always tell the truth. So many people skirt around the truth, or limit its extent as it may make them look bad. Rather than worrying about how you will look, make sure you have the facts straight and be willing to express them.
- Always put the organisation first, then no one can debate your motivation
- Network, network, network. Knowing what makes other people tick helps you to navigate the landscape and allows them to understand you more, which is useful if arguments become heated.
- If you are right, be willing to speak up about it. Rather than wilt if someone attacks you, stand strong and state the facts.
- Help others, be of service to them, and earn their trust and respect
- When dealing with a situation of conflict, mediate by finding common ground. This is the area where everyone can agree to agree. Finding this is the key to disarming politics.
- Also be prepared to agree to disagree. If you are in a deadlocked situation this may be the least preferred alternative, but it may be the only one left.
- Build a reputation for being the peacemaker, someone who can find solutions to difficult problems. This means you rise above politics and become the go-to person to resolve issues in a peaceful way.
- Be prepared to say, 'I don't know.' Especially if you don't have any answers. Don't make something up – just like being honest, being

prepared to say 'I don't know' can also defuse a difficult situation and create an opportunity for action to find out more.
- Be flexible in your approach. Be who you need to be for the situation. You may need to be assertive, or amiable, or on the back foot. The ability to be behaviourally flexible is key to surviving organisational politics.

It takes effort to interact in a politically charged organisation. It can be draining, demoralising, and even overwhelming. Just remember to ease into it and understand the environment before you start playing the game.

The more senior you become, the more likely you will need to learn how to manage politics. I know I spent years avoiding the game and surviving quite well. But it can limit career advancement if you don't have an understanding of how the political game is played.

In a consultant role to a certain organisation, I was required to deal with emotionally charged politics by rolling out a senior program around dealing with change. My political naivety at the time led to incredible feelings of frustration and stress, due to my inability to deal with the politics that underpinned this program.

If I consider each of the points above I probably failed at most of them. I particularly didn't stand strong when I was being personally attacked even though I knew absolutely that I was in the right and doing the right thing. I wilted under pressure and didn't focus on building the necessary relationships to see it through. I persevered and it did go ahead, but with the benefits of hindsight, if I could start that project again I would go about it completely differently!

Some suggestions are:

- Stay true to yourself and trust in your own abilities.
- Take advice only if you have a trusted relationship with the person providing it.
- Go in with your eyes wide open – politics can occur at any time.
- Don't assume you have alliances when you have spent no time creating them.
- Know your facts, and build awareness and understanding of the landscape, the players, and the rules.

My questions are:

- What is your understanding of the organisation you work for?
- Do you understand the underpinning politics?
- Who can you or should you build alliances with for the work you want to do?

In Conclusion

I wrote this book because I want you to believe that you can move up the 'expertise and mindset' model (Figure 1) from wherever you currently are.

We need people like you to step up and own your space. You now understand what you can do differently to lift your career in ways that do not compromise who you are, and help to focus your attention on some small changes you can make.

Focus on:

- Becoming purposeful (Figure 2) and moving to the quadrant of high confidence and high ability. The tools are here to help you move from the quadrant you currently identify with.

- Being self-aware and aware of others and raising your emotional intelligence by being flexible, perceptive and resourceful.

- Being congruent, walking your talk and aligning your head, heart, and gut brains.

- Knowing what you want to achieve – your desired state. For what purpose do you want to achieve that and what is preventing you?

- Creating a well formed outcome for what you do want to achieve.

- Aligning yourself with your strengths and values.

- Being comfortable with change and being out of your comfort zone.

- Putting in the work and practising the exercises to create a high-performance mind.

- Becoming familiar with the impact of the five domains of human social experience: Status, Certainty, Autonomy, Relatedness, and Fairness.

- Pausing when you are confronted with something that you don't like, and considering why.

- Becoming passionate about building rapport with each and every person you communicate with in person, on the phone, or even in written correspondence. Reduce differences at unconscious levels to create a harmonious relationship.

- Building your trust accounts with the people you interact with using the building blocks of trust – capability, communication, and collaboration - and the four elements of personal trust – reliability, acceptance, openness, and congruence.

- Understanding how your corporation works, and connecting into different areas to understand what they do.

- Finding one or two mentors outside of your immediate team

- Raising your awareness of the hierarchy, the silos and the politics that may exist in your organisation.

As I discussed in my introduction, this isn't just about you. This is about creating a large impact on organisations around the world, to create diversity of thought by balancing gender, age, and culture, and creating a lift in what the organisations are offering the world.

I believe that if everyone lifts their confidence and ability even a small amount, the impact on their organisation will be huge.

Let's tap into our untapped talent – that's you. Become instrumental in creating change and bringing much-needed diversity to your organisation

Let's fill organisations with women and men who value being *invested* at 100% and having a mindset of *living to serve*.

Thank you so much for reading this book. Now go out and thrive!

I hope everyone that is reading this is having a really good day. And if you are not, just know that in every new minute that passes you have an opportunity to change that.

—Gillian Anderson

Acknowledgments

I would like to thank my children – Callon and Rhys, who, while not necessarily understanding what I do all the time, totally support me and challenge me everyday to lift my game.

Thank you to my wonderful husband Tony – your ongoing support and the love you show me everyday (as well as taking care of most of the family demands) is why I have been able to write this book.

Many thanks as well to my thought partners and dear friends, who have been with me through thick and thin, saved me from myself a few times, and even let me try out different techniques on them:

- Deb Dalziel
- Tracey Ezard
- Donna McGeorge
- Simone Van Veen

And this book would not have happened without the people I have learnt so much from to get me to this stage:

- Roger Deaner
- Matt Church
- Peter Cook

Thanks.

www.ingramcontent.com/pod-product-compliance
Lightning Source LLC
Chambersburg PA
CBHW071926290426
44110CB00013B/1496